The Devil
You Don't Know

Written in a wonderfully accessible style and drawing on sound pastoral judgment, this is a book less about fascination with the occult and much more about how to deal with the deceptions and discouragements of evil that we all encounter in our everyday lives. This is solid spiritual reading.

Donald Senior, C.P.
President
Catholic Theological Union

With the skill of an experienced spiritual guide, Fr. Louis Cameli unmasks the "ordinary work" of the devil and shows us how new insights into scripture and a deepened friendship with Jesus Christ can assure our perseverance on the journey to the Abba-Mystery of God.

Agnes Cunningham, S.S.C.M.
Professor Emerita
Mundelein Seminary

Louis Cameli's book will be a help to both preachers and spiritual directors to trace destructive patterns as they emerge in an individual's life or in world events.

Daniel Coughlin
Former Chaplain
US House of Representatives

The Devil
You Don't Know

RECOGNIZING and RESISTING EVIL
IN EVERYDAY LIFE

LOUIS J. CAMELI

ave maria press AMP notre dame, indiana

Founded in 1865, Ave Maria Press is a ministry of the United States Province of Holy Cross.

www.avemariapress.com

ISBN-10 1-59471-272-7   ISBN-13 978-1-59471-272-2

Cover and text design by Andy Wagoner.

Printed and bound in the United States of America.

Library of Congress Cataloging-in-Publication Data

Cameli, Louis J. (Louis John)
  The Devil you don't know : recognizing and resisting evil in everyday life / Louis J. Cameli.
    p. cm.
  ISBN-13: 978-1-59471-272-2 (pbk.)
  ISBN-10: 1-59471-272-7 (pbk.)
  1. Devil--Christianity. I. Title.
  BT982.C36 2011
  240--dc23

2011021701

Contents

To those I have served as a priest and
who have taught me to understand
the struggle and the grace
of following Jesus every day,
especially the people of
Divine Savior Parish, Norridge, Illinois

Foreword

In this thoughtful and spiritually insightful description of the presence and the work of the power of evil in our world today, Father Louis Cameli invites us to acknowledge that Satan is a real presence and energy in our world, but not one with whom we may ordinarily be familiar. *The Devil You Don't Know* is an exploration of the signs of the Tempter's activity and a reassurance for us to take heart and to draw courage from the triumph that Christ has already achieved in his definitive defeat of Satan's wiles.

Father Cameli suggests that the signs of the Tempter's ordinary and typical activity can be categorized in four ways: deception, division, diversion, and discouragement. Father Cameli clearly highlights how Satan works in these areas, both in public and private life, to move us away from the God of Love. These four areas may seem unrelated to our notions of the extraordinary signs of demonic activity, but it is in just these ways that the Tempter can manipulate and confuse us in our normal everyday lives. We become divided in mind and heart and most importantly we may even become separated from the God who has fashioned us for himself. We become discouraged in our spiritual lives and may even abandon or pause in our journey of faith.

The Devil You Don't Know is a book for our times. With so much attention focused on the extraordinary events of satanic activity, we might well overlook the ordinary presence of the Tempter—and that is just as he would have us do. When we are unaware, his destructive presence has free reign to work unnoticed but with deadly results. Fortunately, Father Cameli's wise spiritual guidance offers us insight and hope as we seek, in the words of the renewal of our baptismal promises, to "renounce Satan . . . and all his evil works."

Most Reverend Wilton D. Gregory
Archbishop of Atlanta

Introduction

Keep alert. Like a roaring lion your adversary the devil prowls around, looking for someone to devour. Resist him, steadfast in your faith. (1 Peter 5:8–9)

A dead giveaway that people have been away from Church for a *very* long time is a reason that they sometimes provide for their absence, "Oh, I don't go to church because of all that fire and brimstone stuff—all the harping on hell and the devil." In fact, for a long time in most mainline Protestant churches and in the Catholic Church as well, very little has been said about hell and the devil. The topic seems to be out of fashion, nothing to be taken seriously except perhaps for entertainment purposes in Hollywood. So, when I shared with friends and colleagues that I was writing a book about the devil, I immediately saw their puzzled faces that seemed to say, "Why would you ever take up such a project?" I also caught a number of specific questions from them.

As I thought about a way to introduce this book, it occurred to me that the questions I had heard in the process of writing it were probably the same kinds of questions that might interest a reader about to launch into the text. The questions are not theoretical but personal. I mean that they are addressed to me, because friends (and perhaps you as a reader) want to know where I stand on issues that are foundational for what I have written. So, by way of introduction, I will share six questions that I have heard and that seemed to be especially important.

1. Do you really believe in the devil?

Absolutely not. I believe in Jesus Christ, who is the victor over the devil. Biblically, believing means both affirming the truth that God has revealed and relying in trust on God, who has revealed the truth. We cannot, therefore, believe in the devil as we believe in God. On the other hand, the existence of devils and demons belongs to the revealed truth not as independent facts but as realities connected to the triumph of Jesus Christ over sin and death. The *Catechism of the Catholic Church* carefully identifies the devil and demons always in coordination with the history of our salvation in Jesus Christ.[1] The baptismal liturgy offers additional support for the claim that we do not believe directly in the devil as such, but rather we believe in Jesus Christ and, in that belief, know of the devil's existence, work, and aims. The baptismal liturgy asks the candidates for baptism: "Do you believe in God, the Father . . . in Jesus Christ . . . in the Holy Spirit?" The question concerning the devil is not about belief but rather about rejection and renunciation: "Do you reject Satan, father of sin and prince of darkness . . . and all his works, and all his empty promises?"

I think that we can take our understanding of the devil's existence and action a step further. Besides our understanding connected with the larger affirmations of our faith in Jesus Christ and the Church's teaching and liturgical tradition, I would also affirm that we also have direct personal knowledge of the devil's existence and works. This comes to us through reflection on our human condition that is marked by the evil one's troubling presence.

I have come to know, not believe, the devil's existence, works, and aims in three particular ways. Some time ago, I taught a course on the spiritual literature that emerged from the Second World War. The writings put me in touch with the Holocaust, or Shoah, and the Nazi efforts to destroy the Jewish people and to harm so many others as well. Over and over again, as I studied the history and the writings of those caught in this maelstrom, I encountered something or someone who was intelligent, concealed, powerful, and extraordinarily destructive. And whatever or whoever this was exceeded human dimensions in its capacity to bring harm to people and to inspire others to annihilate them. I felt through this study that I had encountered the reality of the devil as a fact of life and human history. In this encounter with history and human suffering, I knew the presence of this being that we call by many names, but whose essence is to be forever the evil one.

In my ministry as a spiritual director, I have accompanied people who have tried to stake out a path of discipleship, to be faithful followers of Jesus Christ. They have invariably encountered hostile forces that would subvert their journey. Sometimes their own internal processes caused them to stumble, but often there was something more than their own spiritual clumsiness. On their journeys, they had—in various forms and ways—encountered an adversary. This is the second way I have come to know the subversive presence of the devil.

Finally, I can say quite honestly that in my own life's journey I have known the presence of the evil one. The destination of my journey— I hope and pray—is God, whom I reach through Jesus Christ his Son and in the power of the Holy Spirit. Along the way, I have met resistances and pulls that would lead me away from the very direction I have embraced. I have struggled, and this struggle has been more than a struggle with myself. In other words, I have met one who seems to want to harm me at the most fundamental level of my life—in my relationship with God. It is not a continuously obsessive or oppressive presence, but it makes me know that I am indeed engaged in a struggle. I need God's help.

In brief, I can say that I do not believe in the devil as I believe in God. I have come to know the existence, presence, works, and destructive aims of the devil in the saving work of Jesus Christ. There are also ways that human history, the spiritual lives of others, and my own spiritual journey verify this evil one we call the devil.

2. Do you believe that the devil is a person? Or, is it better to say that "devil talk" is really symbolic language to speak about the problem of evil?

For people of faith, what constitutes us as real persons is our orientation to God, our steady movement toward the one who is both our origin and our destiny. If that is the case, then the devil cannot be a person. The devil is irrevocably opposed to God and oriented away from God. In fact, in 1973 Joseph Ratzinger wrote in this context: "If one asks whether the devil is a person, then one must in an altogether correct way answer that he is the Un-Person, the disintegration and corruption of what it means to be a person. And so it is particular to him that he moves about without a face and that his inability to be recognized is his actual strength."[2] The engaging figure of Mephistopheles from the story of Faust notwithstanding, the devil really has no personality.

With that understanding of what it means to be a person, I can affirm that the devil is not a person. Still, this fallen creature of God is endowed with intelligence and a will, perverse as it might be. These endowments, it seems to me, make the devil personal if not a fully constituted person. So the biblical witness and our way of talking about the devil can use personal categories. We say "he," although of course the devil has no gender. That "he" gives us some way of indicating the personal dimension of the evil one. Perhaps, it seems to be pure word play to speak of the devil as a personal un-person. But this is much more than playing with words. References to a personal being that is not a person reflect the contradictions and paradoxes that characterize the devil. Created good by God and loved by God, the devil opted against God. Destined by his own decision to remain apart from and alienated from God irrevocably, he cannot remain at peace with his decision but wants to drag all creation, particularly humanity, with him away from God.

The question was whether "devil talk" was symbolic rather than a reference to a real person. The answer is that references to the devil are not just symbolic, although there are symbolic elements in play. The devil, however, is not a person, that is, a being of intelligence and will oriented to God. He does retain elements that make him personal. And that fact may be essential for understanding how he can get to us and hook us. He does so with his intelligence and perverse willfulness.

3.   Aren't you afraid of the devil?

No, I am not afraid of the devil. The words of Jesus in John's Gospel at the Last Supper are very important for me: "Take courage. I have conquered the world" (John 16:33). In this matter of learning not to fear the devil, I have found wonderful instruction in the writings of Saint Teresa of Jesus, who had her own significant struggles with the evil one: "May what was said be of help that the true servant of God might pay no attention to the scarecrows the devil set up in order to cause fear. We should know that each time we pay no attention to them they are weakened, and the soul gains much more mastery."[3]

Although I am not afraid, I try to stay alert, following the injunction that we find in the first letter of Peter: "Keep alert. Like a roaring lion your adversary the devil prowls around, looking for someone to devour. Resist him, steadfast in your faith" (1 Peter 5:8–9). I try to couple alertness with resistance. I do not resist the devil by dint of my own strength, which is completely insufficient. For me, resistance means holding close to faith in Jesus Christ, victor over sin and death. In another way, I try to stay alert especially in spiritual matters by maintaining an attitude of discernment: "Beloved, do not believe every spirit, but test the spirits to see whether they are from God" (1 John 4:1).

I fully agree with Walter Kasper's conclusion: "The basic Christian attitude before the reality of the evil one is not fear but hope in his definitive defeat."[4] In the end, I can say that I am not afraid of the devil, but I do take the reality of the evil one very seriously by being alert, resisting him in faith, discerning all the spiritual impulses I encounter, and returning often to my fundamental hope in Jesus Christ and his victory.

4. *Why did you write this book?*

Throughout my years of service as a priest, I have been especially concerned about Christian formation, both of individuals and church communities. What matters most in Christian formation, that process of our continuing transformation in Christ, is the grace of God. God has been good beyond measure to us, and this is evident in the mystery of Jesus Christ and the gifts of the Holy Spirit that he has poured out upon us. Our first and continuing response must be praise and thanksgiving. At the same time, it would be foolish to think that we have already arrived at our heavenly destination and full transformation in Christ. We are pilgrims who are on the way. As pilgrims we are subject to the trials, struggles, and temptations that accompany us on our journey. Sometimes, we are our own worst enemies. On our own, we subvert the journey, make detours, or even regress. But in addition to our own unsure footing, there is one who wants to pull us away from God and desires our ruin. That is why the Lord Jesus taught us to pray, "Lead us not into temptation, but deliver us from the evil one."

There are many naïve Christians who do not sufficiently take into account the adversary who wishes their destruction. There are also others who only see the work of the devil in spectacular or dramatic ways—demonic possession or signs of the coming of the anti-Christ. More and more, I am convinced that what is needed is a sober Christian realism about the devil and his works. Followers of Jesus need to recognize the ordinary work of the devil that can be so easily insinuated in their daily lives—so seamlessly that it goes unnoticed but is by no means ineffective. I have written this book so that people may appreciate the reality of their daily struggle with the one who would subvert their journey to God. I want them to recognize the daily devil that they did not know.

5. *Did you include any of your personal experiences of the devil in the book?*

Yes, I did. In fact, as I read over what I wrote, I realized that almost every line has an autobiographical quality to it. Whatever is here represents the traditions of faith, my own lived experience, and my pastoral experience. There is nothing here that has not been a part of my own spiritual journey. That is a difficult admission to make, but it is true and humbling. This book falls under the general category of Christian spirituality. And every study of Christian spirituality is self-implicating. I am not writing about the Christian life and its struggles with the devil as if it were outside of me. I am bound to the topic. Perhaps more significantly, we are all bound together in the topic. To write, to read, to study about the dimension of struggle in the Christian life is not about something out there; it is about us. Because of the personal nature of these reflections, I have felt a special responsibility to be genuine and clear. I have tried as best as I could to be transparently honest.

6. *How do you think this book will help people?*

I have some simple hopes for the readers of this book. I hope that in reading it, they may understand their own struggles more clearly. I hope that they will be more alert to what would pull them away from God. I hope that they will learn to be more dependent on Jesus Christ. If these hopes are fulfilled, I will be very happy.

1

The Devil among Us

Fright, Fun, Foreboding

Frightening people makes for good—or, at least, profitable—entertainment. The devil and his cohorts scare people in movies about possession or mysterious forces that can annihilate humanity. Our most primitive fears—being taken over by an alien force, facing our imminent destruction, struggling mightily with negative forces and impulses that well up within us—find expression in evil personified.

Strangely, the very image of the demonic that can be such an effective vehicle for frightening us can also assume a comic form. You can be sure that among the costumed revelers at a Mardi Gras celebration or a Halloween party there will be plenty of "devils" fully vested with horns, tails, and pitchforks.

Fright and fun, however, sometimes give way to a more menacing and truly sad "use" of the devil in our world. Satanist cults and the invocation of dark powers among some, often young, people provide a launching pad for rebellion and mayhem. I do not know if anyone has a clear sense of where this odd and sometimes tragically destructive behavior comes from. Think Charles Manson. Think Columbine. Is it rooted in deep anger and resentment that can be expressed only in negative and destructive energy? Is it connected with a sense of powerlessness that struggles to acquire some control and even mastery in this world? Whatever their psychological or sociological origins, the foreboding Satanist cults use a set of inherited images and symbols to claim power and leave a mark in this world, often a blemish but sometimes a very deep scar. In this sense, so-called Satanist groups use the devil to further their particular cause, not necessarily the devil's.

Whether the devil is employed to entertain us by fright or by clownishness or, more menacingly, to threaten us by his self-designated emissaries, the common thread is drama. The spectacle of diabolical presence and action fascinates us, draws us in, and makes us want to look. That is the dramatic hook of all this devil stuff. It is not, however, the whole story, nor is it the most important part of the story.

There is the ordinary work of the devil and the ordinary presence of the devil. On a daily basis, whether we are conscious or not, we face a formidable adversary who rarely claims a dramatic role in our lives but who, nevertheless, intrudes regularly in ways that are harmful or even destructive. It is worth our while to pay attention.

A Sense of Struggle

We all struggle. I may have a difficult time in getting going on a project or bringing it to completion. I may find a co-worker difficult to work with. Perhaps, a long-time friend becomes tiresome for whatever reason, and it is difficult just to pay attention to ordinary conversation. At times, I feel that I must fight to make myself clear. I strain to get at some elusive truth. I exert every bit of energy within me to calm a troubled situation. I shock myself when I discover inclinations within me toward hostility or even violence, or some form of lust and maybe even a ripe desire to exploit someone for my own satisfaction.

There are a thousand manifestations of struggle, and we know so many of them on a daily basis. Some of these struggles are "local," that is, they belong to me and represent a struggle with myself. The moral dilemma that Saint Paul describes in his letter to the Romans (7:14–21) is a good example: "I can will what is right, but I cannot do it. For I do not do the good I want, but the evil I do not want is what I do" (Romans 7:18b–19).

Struggles, however, are not limited to struggles with myself. Outside forces or agents can conspire to thwart me. The economic system may seem to work against my financial well-being. A mischievous colleague puts out a false report about my job performance. I can be acutely aware that my struggle is with something or someone outside of myself.

More complicated than struggles internal or external are the struggles that lead us to wrestle with what seems to be a mixture of interior and exterior tensions. It is, for example, painfully difficult to know high ideals and great aspirations and, at the same time, to be jarringly aware of the miserable underside of life. To glimpse the true, the beautiful, and the good and then to juxtapose it with the false, the discordant, and the venal—that is a painful struggle to bear, especially for a sensitive heart. No doubt, that is a special struggle for noble souls who have a grand vision for humanity and have daily contact with profound human suffering. I think of people like Mother Teresa and Martin Luther King Jr. and many others like them, although less well-known.

Now, one of the most curious elements of human struggle is how surprising it is. Oddly, although struggle in its various forms belongs to such a wide swath of human experience, its presence still surprises us. Why, we think, do I have to go through this, when I am battling illness or negative impulses or nasty neighbors or oppressive and repressive measures of government? It would seem self-evident that we have to "go through this" just because it is a part of life to struggle, to fight against whatever, and to wrestle with forces within us or outside of us. In other words, we experience what seems to be a natural part of life, struggle, as something that is quite out of place. The fact and experience of struggle jolts us.

At some level of awareness, the adversarial or struggle dimension of life does not make sense. It does not fit our understanding of how life ought to be. The variance between what we experience and what we expect provides a clue for our understanding. We feel that something is amiss. And that feeling finds its roots in a deeper intuition that, indeed, something is wrong. This universal human experience receives a name and some explanation in Christian faith.

What is wrong and should not be wrong, what is wrong and needs to be righted is, in the Christian vision, a good world and a good humanity that early on was marked by sin, a move away from God's original design and destiny for the world and humanity. That is the doctrine of original sin. The original protagonists of original sin are, as the Book of Genesis portrays them, the parents of the human family, Adam and Eve. Their free decision to move away from God's plan for humanity had many consequences. Most notably, it landed us in a state of fractured or split existence. *Homo in seipso divisus est*, says the Second Vatican Council: human beings are divided within themselves.[1] So, the struggle and the roots of the struggle are within us and within the human story.

Now, an important qualification is in order. It might seem that the Christian vision lays all the blame for what went wrong or what is wrong on human beings. If there is evil, it is all our doing. Interestingly, two of the major modern interpretative frameworks for human life and society—Freudian and Marxist theory—do seem to lay all that is bad on the back of either the psyche's self-assertive and self-centered *id* (Freud) or the inevitable social conflicts and inequities of economic systems that set people against each other (Marx). The Christian vision, however, does not see the origin of all evil in humanity.

Certainly, for Christians as for others, human malice is quite capable of extraordinary results that we can categorize as evil. Still, evil—again in a context of faith—antedates the beginnings of humanity. Clearly, this evil is not a contrapuntal force equal to the good God. That is the position of metaphysical dualism that pits a power of good against a power of evil. The evil that antedates humanity belongs to an evil one who most assuredly is not God but was created by God and endowed with intelligence and will. In his (if we can use personification and the masculine gender to speak of this non-human but spiritual being of intelligence and will) rebellion against God, he wants to subvert the whole of creation and drag humanity into this same negative vortex. This is the devil. God permits his acts of subversion, especially by way of temptation but by other means as well, just as God permits you and me to subvert and rebel against God's plan by our sinful behavior. Faith affirms that the last word is God's triumph. Before that, however, there is temptation and sin and evil—all of which must be faced and addressed by people of faith.

Sin, Guilt, and Identity

When the Greeks spoke of sinning, they used the word *hamartein*, which means "to miss the mark." We know that with or without the devil's help, we are quite capable of missing the mark. Our sin has to do with bad behaviors—lying, stealing, hurting, using others, betraying love and friendship, making unjust and unwarranted judgments of others, advancing ourselves at a cost of others' well-being. The list of bad behaviors can go on and on. Sometimes, our sin involves neglecting to do what we ought to do—feeding the hungry from our abundance; stopping to help a hurt person; taking time to support a troubled friend or colleague; taking responsibility for our civic life together so that justice, peace, and harmony might be promoted. Again, the list of possible omissions can stretch quite far.

Sins, as we know them, are acts that we commit or omit. In a sense, these behaviors of commission or omission come from us. They belong to us. And we must assume responsibility for them. At the same time, we do not identify ourselves with our sins. They are like naughty children who belong to us and whom we have generated and for whom we have responsibility. Still, they are not exactly us. They are somehow separate from us. When I confess my sins and seek forgiveness, I say that I have murdered but not that I am murder, that I have lied but not that I am untruth, that I have fornicated but not that I am lust, that I failed to speak up for someone wrongly accused but not that I am injustice or indifference. We are responsible for the sins we commit and the good actions that we ought to do, but we do not define ourselves by them.

There is another level of self-awareness that is not so universally shared, and this self-awareness does have to do with identity. Some of us come to realize not only that we commit sins and omit the good we ought to do, but that we *are sinners*. To say that I am a sinner is to stake a claim about my identity, not what I do or fail to do but *who I am*. How do we experience this identity as sinners?

Almost spontaneously, most people would associate the experience of being a sinner with feelings of guilt. We all feel guilty at various times and in varying degrees, but that feeling does not constitute the experience of being a sinner. In general, guilt is a feeling of remorse for having done something bad or not doing what we should have done. An accurate understanding of guilt feelings is worth the expenditure of some effort, because in so many instances these feelings exercise such a powerful influence in our lives.

Guilt is a feeling, and it is very important to note that. Feelings, especially intense ones, seem like they will last forever. In fact, they are famously transient—here today and gone tomorrow. They can return and sometimes do with a vengeance, but their staying power is always limited. Infatuations and hatreds feel like forever, but the fact is that they eventually pass away, sometimes to return but sometimes not.

At times, guilt is an appropriate and helpful feeling, even if it is transient. We feel bad about what we have done or failed to do, because, indeed, we have done something bad or failed to do the good. The feeling of guilt leads us to seek forgiveness and mend our ways and, as best as we can, to mend the situation as well.

At other times, guilt is an inappropriate and unhelpful feeling. We feel bad for something that is quite out of the range of our responsibility. Survivor's guilt is an example. It is to feel remorse because everyone else in a car accident perished while you alone survived, even though you do not have any real responsibility for the death of others. Often the spouse of an alcoholic has a profound sense of guilt for not being able to stop the alcoholic partner's drinking or for not being able to create the conditions that would obviate the alcoholic's need to drink. In these cases, the feeling does not match the reality and is, therefore, inappropriate. The feeling of guilt in these examples is also unhelpful because it cannot lead to any personal change that would make things right.

A third possibility is the absence of guilt feelings when, in fact, they should be present. Currently, for example, in our culture sex and various forms of sexual acting out have been depersonalized. The flood of advertisements, films, TV shows, and other forms of public communication have trivialized sex. For many people, sex has little to do with sustained commitment, honest and hard-earned intimacy, disciplined fidelity, and openness to generating life. Daily—and on a massive scale—sex is portrayed as entertainment, as recreation, as a game, and as fundamentally inconsequential. Immersion in such a culture with its barrage of messages can easily desensitize people to the gravity of sex and even to the genuine human satisfaction that it affords to those who take it seriously. Consequently, people casually act out sexually, and they feel no guilt. Without the guilt that ought to be a part of their experience, there is no pull to change, to behave differently.

We began by considering the experience of being a sinner—not just someone who commits the bad or omits the good, but someone who experiences being a sinner as a mark of identity. As we try to describe and understand that experience of being a sinner, we readily think that it has to do with feeling guilty. In fact, this is not so. Like all feelings, guilt feelings are transient and, therefore, unable to sustain something that we consider a part of our identity. We also noted that guilt feelings run a gamut of appropriateness and helpfulness. Sometimes, guilt is a genuine consequence of doing the bad or omitting the good, and it is appropriate. Sometimes, guilt is deeply felt but inappropriate because the guilty person thinks he or she is responsible and is not. Sometimes, guilt is not felt, and it should be. Later, these distinctions will serve us as we explore the devil's work in daily life. For now, these distinctions help us to understand that guilt feelings do not precisely define our identity as sinners. There is more to understanding that identity.

We can begin by returning to the earlier question: how do we experience ourselves as sinners, not just as those who commit sins? How does this identity as sinner manifest itself? Obviously, we are dealing with very personal matters. Identity, unless it is affixed to a wide category such as gender, race, ethnicity, or culture, belongs to the individual as such. In other words, I am a sinner in a unique way that belongs specifically to me. I am not a generic sinner, because generic sinners do not exist. It is all quite specific, and this helps to understand why the Catholic tradition insists on individual confession.

Granted the particularity of our identity as sinners, there are, I believe, some common lines of experience that may help us to understand who we are. I can cite at least five such "lines of experience" that help to fill out the picture of being a sinner. Surely, there are other experiential elements, but these may be sufficient to jog our consciousness into a more explicit awareness of this feature of our lives, of who we are.

Distance from Home

A first experience that sinners have is a sense of distance from home. I may be quite comfortable and settled in my current life situation, but a feeling tugs at me. I sense that I have not yet landed, not yet arrived. This very feeling finds expression in the Psalms that echo the words of those in exile. "As a deer longs for flowing streams, so my soul longs for you, O God. . . . When shall I come and behold the face of God?" (Psalm 42:1, 2b). Think, too, of the prodigal son in Jesus' parable (Luke 15:11–32). He not only sinned, he also found himself far from home in foreign territory. The experience of being a sinner includes this sense or feeling, sometimes stronger and more pronounced and at other times less so, of not being at home.

Inner Division

A second marker for the experience of being a sinner is a sense of inner division, a feeling of being divided within ourselves, perhaps, at times even a feeling of a war within. Now, there are genuine psychopathologies that claim people and divide them on the inside so that they cannot function or function very well. That sort of mental illness or dysfunction is not intended here. More commonly, we live our lives without dramatic flourishes. We function well or, at least, sufficiently well. Still, we are also aware of division within us below the surface.

Earlier we cited Saint Paul, who voiced this experience: "I do not understand my own actions. For I do not do what I want, but I do the very thing I hate" (Romans 7:15). Like Paul, we know a gap between our aspirations and our possibilities. And we know that gap is somehow rooted on the inside, in our divided hearts that we have no control over. The inner division of sinners restricts the flow of love and good that could emanate from us. We may not understand this, but we do know that it is true.

Interior Woundedness

An interior woundedness is a third marker of the experience of being a sinner. Feeling wounded differs from feeling interiorly divided. The wounded person feels pain and perhaps weakness. The wounded person senses a need for healing to stop the pain and to gain strength. A vivid expression of this interior woundedness comes to us in the Psalms: "For my days pass away like smoke, and my bones burn like a furnace. My heart is stricken and withered like grass; I am too wasted to eat my bread. Because of my loud groaning my bones cling to my skin" (Psalm 102:3–5). These words express an acute experience of an inner wound or sickness that needs healing. Many of us can more readily identify a more general aching feeling that things are not right and need healing.

A Sense of Burden

A fourth marker of the experience of being a sinner is a sense of burden. In other words, we find ourselves carrying things within ourselves that weigh us down and leave us with diminished freedom. The burden may assume various forms, such as old resentments, personal rejection, fears that the past will return to haunt us, anxieties about the next step in our lives or the future more generally, others' unreasonable expectations of us that we have made our own, and repetitive self-destructive or self-diminishing patterns of behavior that make up the stuff of addictions. The essential element of this sense of burden is that it takes away our freedom, our essential freedom to be ourselves. We long to have the weight lifted and to move freely.

Longing for Love

A fifth and final marker of the experience of being a sinner is longing for a love that is complete but seemingly out of reach. We want to love and to be loved. We intuit the fullness of this love, its absolute and commanding presence that makes everything else make sense. Still, even with the intuition of this love's presence, we know that we do not have it and perhaps cannot have it. The variance between the love we were made for and its lack of attainment pains us. We know that we are made for—destined for—a love that we have not attained.

These are some of the experiential markers of being a sinner, of having the identity of being a sinner, not just one who commits sin. They are a felt distance from home, an inner division, an interior woundedness, a sense of burden that leaves us unfree, and a longing for the fullness of love not yet attained. The net impact of these experiences and this identity as sinner is to leave us vulnerable to the incursions of the evil one. For whatever else can be said about our identity as sinners, surely the most significant is that it stakes us off as not fully and definitively saved, at best, on our way to the full salvation that lies ahead. We exist provisionally. We have not yet arrived. We may be saved, but, as Saint Paul reminds us, "we are saved in hope" (Romans 8:24). On the way home, moving toward an inner unity, working toward healing for what ails us, marching toward freedom from our personal burdens, and walking toward the fullness of love—all this leaves us vulnerable. We can go off course. And there is malevolence that wants these poor sinners who aspire to be saints to be subverted on their journey and rerouted to an unholy destination.

Now, we are ready to understand how the devil works in ordinary ways in the course of ordinary life. We can identify the daily devil that we did not know.

2

The Ordinary Work of the Devil:

Deception

You are from your father the devil, and you choose to do your father's desires. He was a murderer from the beginning and does not stand in the truth, because there is no truth in him. When he lies, he speaks according to his own nature, for he is a liar and the father of lies. (John 8:44)

Reality Inverted and False Promises

The devil inverts reality, that is, he turns things inside out, upside down. Then he proceeds to present the inversion as the honest-to-God truth. In other words, he lies. Often, this lie has to do with a promise that, of course, can never and will never be kept. We human beings, however, are a gullible lot. And from the beginning, we have been suckers for empty promises cooked up in a pot of lies.

The devil uses deceitful promises to tempt us, to pull us off track. This is hardly new. The first and eternally paradigmatic instance of this ploy can be found in the beginning of the Book of Genesis: "But the serpent said to the woman, 'You will not die; for God knows that when you eat of it your eyes will be opened, and you will be like God, knowing good and evil'" (Genesis 3:4–5). Here, the lie works. In another well-known instance of a temptation embedded in a deceitful promise, the devil does not succeed at all. In the third temptation of Jesus in Matthew's Gospel, we read:

> Again, the devil took him to a very high mountain and showed him all the kingdoms of the world and their splendor; and he said to him, "All these I will give you, if you will fall down and worship me." Jesus said to him, "Away with you, Satan! For it is written, 'Worship the Lord your God, and serve only him.'" Then the devil left him, and suddenly angels came and waited on him. (4:8–11)

Notice that these deceitful promises, rooted in lies, have to do with the future. There is something ahead, the devil seems to say, that I can assure you will be to your liking and will suit you well. Promised futures, assured results, controlled outcomes—these all lure us powerfully. It *feels* much better to think that we know how things will turn out, even if this feeling is based on something that is untested and, ultimately, untrue. It feels better to move forward with some measure of control rather than to walk with trust and hope and have little or no control over what will happen.

So often the devil's deception is attached to a promise that, of course, has to do with the future. That ought to alert us to be on guard when we look ahead, when we are making plans, or when we are daydreaming about what could be. C. S. Lewis had his devil, Screwtape, make this observation: "Nearly all vices are rooted in the Future. Gratitude looks to the Past and love to the Present; fear, avarice, lust, and ambition look ahead. Do not think lust an exception. When the present pleasure arrives, the sin (which alone interests us) is already over."[1] All this means that we suffer a kind of vulnerability to deception as we anticipate what might be ahead. Deceptions can, of course, be about a thousand things: how much I would enjoy a sexual relationship with so and so, how well I would live with extra money in my pockets, how satisfied I would be if I got the promotion instead of my colleague, how secure I would feel if I could only grab that business opportunity, how satisfied I would be to live in that neighborhood. These speculations reflect a kind of future payoff.

There are also other assurances about the future, equally deceptive, that falsely promise to conceal what we would rather have kept secret. The desire to maintain privacy in one's life has an absolutely positive ring to it. We think of privacy as a form of legitimate reserve that holds to oneself what would otherwise be indelicately or rudely shared with a larger public. Although an earlier age may have equated privacy with refinement, today privacy has a less seemly aspect. For many, privacy means blocking off parts of their life that they just want to keep to themselves, generally because they are not proud of their actions or they fear that these actions may rebound in a negative way and interrupt their life. There are many things people might want to block off: use of pornography, propensity to take things that do not belong to them from work, a regular habit of ignoring appeals for help, episodes of drug and alcohol abuse, and cheating in school and on taxes. And where does the devil enter into these private matters? The devil is active in several ways. The very strategy of blocking off or bracketing for the sake of deceptive concealment belongs in a notable way to the evil one.

Saint Ignatius of Loyola describes this phenomenon in *The Spiritual Exercises* in his rules for the discernment of spirits. He writes:

> Our enemy may also be compared in his manner of acting to a false lover. He seeks to remain hidden and does not want to be discovered. If such a lover speaks with evil intention to the daughter of a good father, or to the wife of a good husband, and seeks to seduce them, he wants his words and solicitations kept secret. He is greatly displeased if his evil suggestions and depraved intentions are revealed by the daughter to her father, or by the wife to her husband. Then he readily sees he will not succeed in what he has begun. In the same way, when the enemy of our human nature tempts a just soul with his wiles and seductions, he earnestly desires that they be received secretly and kept secret. But if one manifests them to a confessor, or

> to some other spiritual person who understands his deceits
> and malicious designs, the evil one is very much vexed. For
> he knows that he cannot succeed in his evil undertaking,
> once his evident deceits have been revealed.[2]

In addition to the very strategy of deceptive concealment, the devil offers a promise and (again deceptively) mitigates the evil that he offers as a temptation. The promise is simply that the evil will not be known, and the mitigation is that it really does not matter that much in any case. The promise is false, and the statement of mitigation is also false. If it is to the advantage of the evil one to make known what might otherwise be a hidden fault or failure, he will surely make it known. He can thereby mislead others, provoke scandal, and cause the person so exposed to be hurled into the throes of destructive depression. This is exactly the case with the tragic stories of clerical sexual misconduct with minors. What seemed to have been sealed shut, out of public view, by personal shame and institutional connivance at a certain point surfaced rapidly and forcefully to mislead people about the Church by provoking scandal after scandal, one stumbling block upon another. The shameful truth made public also unleashed waves of destructive depression among perpetrators, victims, and countless good and trusting souls in the Church.

The claim of mitigation in the case of clerical sexual misconduct, but also in other instances of hidden evil, "It does not make that much difference," clearly revealed itself as false. Whether evil is public or putatively private and hidden, it has an impact, and it exacts a price. Our deep human connections and our solidarity in the human condition and human history inevitably link our most "private" behavior with some form of impact on others. We are too connected to each other and so interdependent that we can never seal ourselves off from the rest of humanity, either in our impact on others or their impact on us.

By way of summary, we can make a simple statement. The devil does not keep his promises because he is deceptive. To identify this fact, however, does not automatically free us from the influence of the one who habitually inverts the truth and seeks to entwine us in his distortions. We remain vulnerable and, therefore, must also remain alert.

Complicated Tangles: The Stuff of Deception

Mark's Gospel describes an extraordinary debate that Jesus has with the Sadducees about the resurrection of the dead. Here is the text:

> Some Sadducees, who say there is no resurrection, came to him and asked him a question, saying, "Teacher, Moses wrote for us that if a man's brother died, leaving a wife but no child, the man shall marry the widow and raise up children for his brother. There were seven brothers; the first married and, when he died, left no children; and the second married her and died, leaving no children; and the third likewise; none of the seven left children. Last of all, the woman herself died. In the resurrection whose wife will she be? For the seven had married her." Jesus said to them, "Is not this the reason you are wrong, that you know neither the scriptures nor the power of God? For when they rise from the dead, they neither marry nor are given in marriage, but are like angels in heaven. And as for the dead being raised, have you not read in the book of Moses, in the story about the bush, how God said to him, 'I am the God of Abraham, the God of Isaac, and the God of Jacob'? He is not God of the dead, but of the living; you are quite wrong." (12:18–27)

This passage reflects a strategy used by the Sadducees to discredit Jesus. The complicated tangles of the story that the Sadducees present in the text are not meant, as they might be in a good-faith disputation, to be unraveled to arrive at a truth about the resurrection of the dead. Instead, the complications are designed to disguise and conceal a fundamental truth—that God is God of the living and not of the dead. Jesus uses the plain and simple statement of this truth to cut through the complicated sophistries latent in the case that the Sadducees present. The argument of the Sadducees does not lead to truth, but away from truth. The Sadducees accomplish this by layering a narrative with a complicated mixture of law (the obligation of a brother to raise up children to his deceased brother's name), speculation about the afterlife ("Whose wife will she be?"), and the implicit imposition of limits on God, the very creator and sustainer of human life ("you know neither the scriptures nor the power of God"). This complicated and convoluted approach attempts to disguise the truth of God's power and the foundation of the resurrection of the dead. Jesus' response to this argument is not to engage the Sadducees in their concealment of the truth by way of complications that obscure. Rather, he proposes plainly and simply what lies inside the tangle of complexity: God is God, not of the dead but of the living.

The complications of presentation, logic, and argumentation that the evil one employs to conceal the simple truth are not to be confused with what is difficult to understand. Because I am not trained in higher mathematics, various number theories seem to me to be complicated and impossible to decipher. The same could be said of other areas studied by the natural sciences from astrophysics to nuclear physics. The difficulty of understanding is inherent in the material that needs to be studied. And it is studied precisely because there is an intelligibility, a capacity to be known and understood with the proper and sufficient tools of thought and analysis. Otherwise, there would be no science but just perpetual puzzlement.

The complicated tangles that are related to deception have to do with a free choice to make things complicated so that they can be obscured and, ultimately, be part of the deception. In this, we see the hand of the evil one—intelligence coupled with malevolent will.

Think of a shell game. The sleight of hand moves the shells quickly here and there, attempting—with complicated motions—to distract viewers and to obscure the exact position of the object under the shell and so deceive the participants who gamble their money, wagering that they know the truth under the shells. In a simple game, this kind of complicated tangle may have minimal impact—perhaps the loss of a limited amount of money. The stakes, however, can be much higher—and the deception by way of complication can be much more lucrative—when it is played out on a grander scale: for example, in the derivatives market, a way of making money that scarcely anyone seems to understand. It entails the selling of mortgage obligations to others who hold the debt and who, in turn, sell it to others, and so on. The complexities of this market are such that government regulators are at a loss to determine how to monitor and control this lucrative but thoroughly unstable trading. When an investment in the derivatives market goes bad, the net effect is to produce catastrophic losses. A buyer's greed coupled with a seller's capacity to "keep the shells moving rapidly" can combine to develop into a perfect storm of losses for investors. Tangled complications create deception, which, in turn, devolves into loss.

Of course, the devil is quite capable of bringing confusing complexities into our personal lives and so tries to conceal the truth of who we are or the authentic call that God gives us. Various overlays, for example, questioning our motivations, raising concerns about others' perceptions of us and our projects, projecting all the possible difficulties we might face—all these serve to block us or, at least, make us stumble on our journey by injecting deceit by way of complications.

Although the devil can and, indeed, does take this approach to deception in dealing with individuals, I am convinced that the driving spirit of complicating to deceive is especially effective in derailing works of justice and peace on a larger scale of community and systems. Two examples drawn from current political and social life in the United States come to mind: providing universal health care and reforming immigration law. Both of these issues have to do with basic life issues, with promoting human dignity, and with living out what ought to be our fundamental national commitments to justice and peace. As we approach these issues, however, even at the level of preliminary national discussion and debate, complications of such a magnitude become evident that the projects of health care and immigration reform seem to be completely out of reach. Universal health care will be too expensive. We do not know how the public and private sectors will manage in the context of universal care. We will all, in some measure, be denied a level or quality of care. And concerning immigration reform, we cannot open our borders to potential terrorists or to the exploitations of common criminals. Sectors of the economy may depend on the labor of illegal immigrants, but we do not want to endorse lawbreaking. The complications are endless, and a social paralysis can easily set in. We anticipate failure even before we make any attempts to address the issues. We feel pulled in the direction of doing nothing because nothing can be done. And this is an evil direction, because it surrenders the fate of vulnerable and marginalized people to blind market forces or nationalistic-nativist rhetoric.

In the midst of significant complications, simple and plain truths can and ought to be evident. Human beings have an inherent dignity. Those who are sick or in any way vulnerable deserve our special concern and consideration. The devil, however, is the sworn enemy of the plain and simple truth. Because it is plain and simple, the truth will be known and will be a path to God, who is truth. The enemy will always be interested in concealing the truth with complexities that do not allow us to view it, deal with it, or even speak about it sensibly.

Expressiveness versus Disclosure: A Deceptive Semblance of Truth

Deciphering the meaning and depth of communication in different cultures remains a challenge for most people. In some cultures, for example, expressiveness, an effusive style of language and gesture, suggests to those not accustomed to this style that the speaker is disclosing or revealing something of the self at quite a personal depth. In fact, this may not be the case at all. Expressiveness is not an automatic pass-key to self-disclosure. In fact, an intensely expressive style in language and gesture may effectively mask the deeper realties. In certain instances and in some cultural circumstances, however, expressiveness can be a vehicle of self-disclosure. In itself, expressiveness is no guarantee of inner truth. The evil one uses this ambivalence for deceptive purposes.

A most interesting instance of the devil's use of expressiveness to hide the truth has to do with religion. The devil can and does orchestrate religious observances, not, of course, for a positive purpose. He leads worshippers to intense and extensive expressions of religious activity that have little to do with an interiorized and genuine faith. The prophetic tradition in the Bible often critiques this kind of external religious expression to which there is no corresponding interiorized faith. A well-known passage from the prophet Isaiah can serve as an apt example of external and expressive religious behavior masking a dearth of inner commitment. People who engage in this kind of worship, according to the prophet, do not fool themselves and, certainly, do not fool God. We read:

> Why do we fast, but you do not see? Why humble ourselves, but you do not notice? Look, you serve your own interest on your fast day, and oppress all your workers. Look, you fast only to quarrel and to fight and to strike with a wicked fist. Such fasting as you do today will not make your voice heard on high. Is such a fast that I choose a day to humble oneself? Is it to bow down the head like a bulrush, and to lie in sackcloth and ashes? Will you call this a fast, a day acceptable to the Lord? Is not this the fast that I choose: to loose the bonds of injustice, to undo the thongs of the yoke, to let the oppressed go free, and to break every yoke? Is it not to share your bread with the hungry, and bring the homeless poor into your house; when you see the naked, to cover them, and not to hide yourself from your own kin? (Isaiah 58:3–7)

In his preaching and teaching, Jesus continues the prophetic critique of external expressions of religiosity split from interior commitment and so embodying a deception, a lie.

> So the Pharisees and the scribes asked him, "Why do your disciples not live according to the tradition of the elders, but eat with defiled hands?" He said to them, "Isaiah prophesied rightly about you hypocrites, as it is written, 'This people honors me with their lips, but their hearts are far from me; in vain do they worship, teaching human precepts as doctrines.' You abandon the commandment of God and hold to human tradition." (Mark 7:5–8)

And later, speaking of some scribes, he says: "They devour widows' houses and for the sake of appearance say long prayers. They will receive the greater condemnation" (Mark 12:40).

The deceptive tactics of the devil include, then, a pernicious encouragement of religious practices as purely external observances without a corresponding interior commitment. The practices in themselves may be quite legitimate and good. If they are not grounded in an interior commitment, however, they serve as a vehicle of deception. And they are empty shells. Traditionally, wise spiritual directors have always tried to moderate the religious practice of newly fervent people, insisting as they do so that religious or spiritual practice is not so much a matter of quantity and felt intensity, but of authentic, deeply committed worship in spirit and in truth.

Another significant arena for confusing expressiveness with genuine self-disclosure is that of human sexuality. Expressions of intimacy, for example, do not necessarily constitute genuine intimacy between persons. Human sexuality provides a very strong energy for outward expressions that speak of intimacy by way of close physical contact and intense emotional states. Still, that energy and its various external manifestations do not guarantee a genuinely intimate relationship. Genuine intimacy depends on a shared vulnerability that comes with a deliberate and significant investment in mutual self-disclosure. That is a costly process that moves well beyond the surface of a relationship. Ultimately, it depends on commitment and fidelity. In other words, what bonds persons together, and intimately so, is beyond physical coupling. Real connection includes a coming together of the interior, spiritual existence of persons. An intense and fundamentally physical connection can seem to be intimate without, in fact, being so.

The devil can freely use the ambiguity of a physical sexual relationship for his own purposes, which are directed to deceit and, ultimately, to move people off course in their journey to God. Pure lust—the exploitation of another for one's own gratification—clearly speaks the language of self-centeredness. Although pure lust framed in this way does not have the cachet of other more subtle behavior, some do make this their choice. When this choice is made, a blatant moral flaw or shortcoming becomes evident. Another path is possible. The more subtle temptation and direction follows the direction of an apparently intimate relationship, at least externally expressed and seen that way, but which, in fact, is far from genuinely intimate. External expression replaces deeper substance. This happens, for example, in the case of an unmarried cohabiting couple. They are not promiscuous, and, therefore, would not evaluate themselves as "lustful." They would not see their relationship as mutually exploitative. Rather, they experience—by their own account—a deep intimacy based on the external, physical expressions that they share. Because their commitment to each other lacks a binding pledge of fidelity and lifelong communion, it is circumscribed, limited, and provisional. The expression of their physical closeness does not represent or express a deeper intimacy, because it lacks the full commitment that alone can be the foundation of true and full intimacy. Again, external expression replaces the truth of substance.

The demonic ploy, in this context and these examples, is not to tempt people to an illicit sexual engagement, although that surely remains his tactic on occasion. Rather, the tempter uses sexual possibilities to draw people into an unreal world in which they live and experience a semblance of truth, but not the real truth of themselves and others. This fact may explain why so many failed relationships based principally on physical connection end in raging disappointment and a sense of having been deceived and tricked.

A third arena of human life that finds itself easily susceptible to confusing expressiveness and disclosure is political life. Successful politicians are able to communicate well. They have powers of expression and persuasion that enable them to connect with a public. Politicians aim to elicit trust from those who elect them to office. With the people's votes and their trust, politicians who have become elected officials try to advance the programs that will make society peaceful and prosperous. In other words, they advance policies that foster a forward movement of social organization and the quality of life.

For politics to work well for society, it is essential that the common good be of paramount importance. It is also essential that in political speech, expression and disclosure correspond to each other. The common good and honest political discourse are closely related to each other. They can, however, be separated and manipulated in an evil way. Here is how that happens.

At a notional level, everyone would agree that the true common good must be of paramount importance. If, in fact, anything less than the common good commands attention in the political process, then various forms of corruption ensue. Among politicians and elected officials, the devil can appeal to greed, a thirst for power, or a desire for acclaim in such a way that those tempted can manipulate and reshape the common good to fit their aspirations. No politician or elected official would publicly embrace a diminished common good. In other words, it would be political suicide to have one's aspirations for money, power, or acclaim to be clearly visible to the public. To continue one's political ambitions in the context of an altered and diminished common good, a politician or public servant must acquire the habit of expressing one thing, the common good, and not disclosing the deeper truth of personal ambition. Such a habit means perpetual dissimulation, never matching external expression with inner reality.

Political life provides fertile territory for the evil one to bring deceit into a wide range of public life through the political process. Politicians are by profession engaged in expression. In a given society, they are often the communicators *par excellence*. If they speak but do not disclose, if they communicate but do not reveal the substance of political or social realities, then they are easily ensnared by the evil one.

Three significant sectors of human life—religion, sex, and politics—demonstrate a susceptibility to the evil one's deceptive manipulations. The devil's advantage and our disadvantage is the indirectness of the deceptions. A lie is a lie is a lie. It stands out clearly. In the matter of external expression that is accompanied by a failure to disclose inner realities, things are not so simple. It is easier to be taken in by verbiage that hides the inner realities than by a direct act of deceit. In the matter of deception, as we have already seen, the devil is an effective master of subtlety.

A Thoroughly Modern Deception: Information Instead of Truth

It is commonplace to say that we belong to an information-driven society. We do, and the proof of it is evident in the dominance of computers in our society. Computers store and process information, bits and pieces of data. When managed well, the information yields amazing results. Businesses run more efficiently. Manufacturing processes boost their productivity. Schedules are better synchronized. People have more access to each other and can be in more frequent communication. Scholars have easier access to research materials. Prospects for marketing and selling merchandise are greatly expanded. The list could go on and on. The conclusion is that in so many ways because of information technology, we have all benefited and stand to benefit in the future. So, the understandable reaction to all this information and information technology is to applaud the accomplishments. I do believe that affirmation is in order. Many good things have happened because we have access to so much information and to its management. Still, an important word of qualification and caution needs to be offered.

Information as such has both obvious benefits and certain inherent limitations. The more information we have, the better our possibilities for managing our lives and for living more efficiently. Information can certainly help us to live better. Information, however, cannot do everything. Although it may enhance our efficiency and productivity, information cannot give us an answer to the most fundamental questions of life: not simply how we can live, but why we should live; not only how we can live life more efficiently, but what our purpose is on earth; not only how we can know life as a given, but how we can and ought to shape it through our free decisions; not only what the facts of our existence are, but what we can live for and even die for. These contrasts indicate what information *cannot* do. Implicit in all the contrasts is a fundamental contrast between information and truth. Only truth—the truth of our lives and of the world—can adequately address our reasons for existing, our purpose, our freedom, and our most fundamental commitments.

The truth of our lives is not tied into bits and pieces of information, which can be shuffled and manipulated in numerous directions. The truth of our lives is manifest in our identity, that stable sense of self that begins at birth and accompanies us throughout life until we come to the moment of our last breath. The truth of our lives emerges in our core freedom. We certainly do not enjoy absolute freedom. Ours is a freedom that is conditioned and limited in various ways. There is, nonetheless, a core of freedom that enables us not just to make choices, but to give ourselves to others in love (or to refuse to do so) and to affirm our existence as a gift beyond our making (or to refuse to do so). The truth that makes us free leads us to truth itself, truth beyond our imagining, transcendent truth that grounds all truth. And that is God.

If all truth is ultimately grounded in God, who is truth, how does information, which is not truth, fit or not fit with our journey to God? A first and positive observation is in order. The explosion of information and information technology that we are experiencing in an unprecedented way is—from a spiritual perspective—filled with good and even graced possibility. Information and its uses enable us to exercise a stewardship of this world and the goods of our lives. Information and information technology can enable us to connect with each other, creating a web of connections around the globe that the French Jesuit paleontologist Teilhard de Chardin presciently named the noosphere, a mind-web that would envelop the earth just as the biosphere had done. Information and information technology can enable us to create and distribute goods more easily and more fairly and contribute to an overall increase in the quality of life for all people. Information and information technology can contribute to the development of our political and social life. The sharing of information and use of information for social organization can be of great benefit in organizing our lives together.

The positive directions of information and information technology do not automatically flow from the information itself. Information needs guidance by truth and values. The positive possibilities of information can easily be undermined in several ways. And this prompts us to identify how the evil one can use information and information technology for his fundamental purpose, which, of course, is to move us away from our journey to God.

Information and information technology that supplants truth or ignores guidance by truth is deceptive and perilous. When the bits and pieces of information masquerade as truth, things do indeed take a dangerous turn. This is ready terrain for the devil's action. And it deserves special attention, because the challenges of information and information technology are new, and in some measure, our perceptions and defenses are not so well developed to meet these challenges.

Information is fascinating. It draws our attention because we are curious about so many things and so many people. In fact, our fascination with information easily moves to our absorption in it. There is a way—and not limited to information geeks—that information in its various forms can fully absorb us. Absorption means spending time, money, and energy. Market forces recognize this human propensity to be absorbed by information, and they exploit it for a profit. At this point, our fascination with information and even our absorption in it may be quite neutral. No alarms go off. Another, deeper look does suggest grounds for concern.

A significant reason for our fascination with information and even our absorption in it has to do with the sense of control that information seems to impart to us. In fact, having information and using information can enable us to achieve outcomes that might otherwise be out of our reach without the requisite information. If "having control" means the more efficient management of legitimate tasks entrusted to us, then the control afforded by information is good. If "having control" with the use of information means that we can manipulate others and situations for our own self-enclosed purposes, then it is not good. The temptation to use information in this controlling and negative way can exercise a powerful draw by imparting to us an apparent sense of our autonomy and freedom. Ultimately, control exercised in this way leads to human and organizational wreckage. Short-term, it exercises a powerful allure. The fundamental issue is the suppression of the truth of ourselves, our purpose, and our world in the process of trying to seize control by the manipulation of information.

The mix-up and confusion of truth and information reach into very personal dimensions of life. Today's computerized social networks open up undreamed possibilities for human connection. That represents a fundamental human good. There is, however, a potential for misunderstanding and misuse in social networking. The computerized presentation of people to each other basically offers *information about* people and not the *truth of* people. Information about people identifies characteristics of race, ethnicity, culture, physical type, age, and gender as well as particular interests, activities, and decisive life events. This information often seems to generate a portrait of the person, although, in fact, a true picture can never emerge from these bits and pieces. The real person, the truth of the person, cannot be contained in pieces of information. The truth of a person emerges only with a sense of that person's origin and destiny and fundamental commitments, especially of love. In this sense, hyphenated identities, such as Hispanic-Catholic, gay-American, woman-writer, seem to get at the truth of the person, but, in fact, do not. They simply add information that may or may not draw us into the truth of the person so designated.

The devil can readily use this confusion between information about people and the truth of people to great advantage in sowing seeds of disharmony and even deep antagonism. For example, information about people that poses as an expression of their true essence can reinforce prejudices and stereotypical thinking. All manner of nasty thinking and unwarranted assessments of others are possible with this mix-up. From this confusion of information and truth stem racism, sexism, homophobia, classism, national chauvinism, and ethnocentrism. The consistent pattern in these reductive assessments of others is the confusion between information about people, the always partial elements of their characteristics or features, with their fundamental truth, that is, their deep origin, destiny, and commitment-based identity. Clearly, the confusion of information with truth—on a personal level—is a very effective demonic instrument for setting people at odds with each other. And the modern paradox is that what would seem so helpful for bringing us together (for example, computerized social networking and the sharing of information about each other) can be a potent force for driving us apart from each other.

Deceptions and Lies: Remedies for Pain

The old manuals of moral theology referred to a *mendacium jocosum*, literally, a joking lie. This kind of lie with its transparent falsity and evident exaggeration is meant to evoke a laugh and not to fool anyone. The *mendacium jocosum* does not qualify as a sin. At the very most, it may be a bad joke. Real deceptions and real lies have little to do with humor. Real lies and deceptions are fundamentally about pain.

The evil one moves us to tell a lie either to avoid pain or to find relief from pain. On the lower end of the scale of deception, some people lie about their age. Why? To deal with the pain of getting older and all that entails. Someone may lie to a friend about a "previous commitment" to avoid the pain of enduring a boring social engagement. A taxpayer may lie about expenses to avoid the pain of paying out money. Someone may lie about her accomplishments to relieve the pain of her life of disappointments and a low sense of self-worth. An adulterous spouse may lie about his affair to avoid the pain of honest admission and also to avoid the pain that his betrayal would impose on his wife. A government agency might lie about its internal corruption to avoid the pain of exposure, punishment, and reorganization. A government might propose a big lie, as the Nazi regime in Germany did concerning Jews, to relieve the pain of economic hardships and national humiliation. At every level and with varying degrees of gravity, the lies and deceptions of this world are a remedy for pain.

If lies, indeed, have to do with avoiding or relieving pain, then they fall under the category of evasive strategies. Rather than face the pain directly or apply a remedy that directly addresses the pain, the deceptive approach moves obliquely, trying to avoid whatever would hurt. The indirectness of these evasive strategies suggests an easier path, a less demanding way. In fact, the opposite is true. More energy is expended in bending the truth than in dealing with it directly. Often, experience sadly tells us, one lie requires yet another and perhaps another after that. The suggestion of an "easier" way around the truth is an assumption fostered by the evil one to make lying or deceiving a more attractive option.

The devil fosters other assumptions about lies and deception because it is in his interest to make this strategy an appealing one. For example, a fundamental assumption that encourages lying is that the truth is to be feared. When people are afraid of the truth, whatever that truth might be, they will avoid it as if it were a mean and growling dog. The fear of the truth has to do fundamentally with a fear of consequences. If I face up to the truth, what will happen to me? Will that growling dog bite me if I walk up and stand directly before it? As long as I am afraid, I am inclined to deal with my fear rather than with the truth. It is an easy step from fear to deception.

Another assumption encouraged by the devil has to do with the normalcy of deceiving and lying. This is the familiar bromide of "everyone does it." In a culture of deceit, when major institutions of public life—government, manufacturing, banking, media, even churches—are known for employing deceit for profit or protection, it is easy for individuals to be persuaded that lying is a normal part of life.

A more subtle assumption—important for sensitive souls—is that lies inflict less pain than the pain that they seek to address. In other words, better to lie even if there are some painful consequences, because the unvarnished truth will be even more painful. The subtlety of this assumption makes it difficult to address, especially in the minds of those confronted with the temptation to deceive or lie in the context of difficult situations. It seems good or, at least, better to soften the pain, even if that means deception. In fact, things do not work that way. The difficulty stems from the corrosive nature of a lie. At a number of levels and with varying degrees of intensity, a lie wears away the trust that cements human relationships. The lie undermines reliability. Still, in a difficult moment, the prospect of lesser pain provides an often compelling rationale for deception.

A final assumption about lies and deceptions is that lies work—that they are effective in doing what they purport to do, namely, to hide the truth, to create another version of reality, to protect people, and to soften the harsh realities of life. This assumption itself is false. In a long-term context, lies do not work. In fact, again in a long-term context, they cannot work. Lies are constructions of reality. They build foundations on air, because they do not have the solidity of real truth. At some point, anything built on such insubstantial foundations will come crashing down. And that is the pattern that human experience verifies. All this is anticipated in the story of the Fall in Genesis 3. The fundamental lie that the devil proposes to Adam and Eve is "You shall be like gods." They fall for it. As soon as they begin to build their existence on this insubstantial promise, this empty lie, their lives fall apart. They find themselves outside of paradise.

The protective lie, the lie designed to shield oneself or others from pain, neither protects nor shields anyone. Initially, it appears convenient, but it becomes more and more complicated with the passage of time and the need for reinforcing lies. It assumes that the truth is unmanageable, that lies produce less pain than the pain they address, that lies require less energy, that lies are a normal part of life, and that lies work effectively. These are powerful assumptions that provide the evil one with tools to encourage others in his campaign of temptation and of involving others in his fundamentally deceptive practices. In fact, the assumptions are all uniformly false. So, it is a matter of deception building on deception.

Later, in another context, we will consider the temptations of Jesus as an example of the devil's work of diversion, that is, the devil's attempt to divert Jesus from his true mission. We can also read the temptations of Jesus as an example of a protective lie. The tempter's message is "Spare yourself the pain. You need not be the suffering messiah, the one who bears humanity's infirmities. You need not empty yourself to the point of dying on the cross. You can bend your identity as messiah and avoid the mess of betrayal, abandonment, torture, injustice, humiliation, and death as a common criminal on a cross. You can take the pain out of redemption. After all, you are the Son of God, are you not? Cannot the Son of God shape the way he will save the world? See, here. Spare yourself hunger and make these stones bread. Take over all the kingdoms of the earth with a simple submission—no, not even that—but with an acknowledgement of my power over the world. Throw yourself down from the top of the temple and let angels catch you. Then, they will believe in you. Then, they will follow you."

The devil's deception offers a remedy for pain. It follows a compelling logic of convenience, the possibility of an easier route. And this is a real temptation, a real offer and possibility. We know that from a remarkable passage from the Letter to the Hebrews: "For we do not have a high priest who is unable to sympathize with our weaknesses, but we have one who in every respect has been tested as we are, yet without sin" (4:15). We also know that this temptation played out in different ways punctuates the ministry and life of Jesus to the end. In the garden the night before he dies, he grapples again with the temptation: "My Father, if it is possible, let this cup pass from me; yet not what I want but what you want" (Matthew 26:39). In John's Gospel, Jesus speaks of his impending death this way: "Now my soul is troubled. And what should I say—'Father, save me from this hour'? No, it is for this reason that I have come to this hour" (12:27).

Remarkably, this temptation to evade the true path of the messiah, who is God's suffering servant, in favor of an easier, less painful way finds a voice among Jesus' closest followers and collaborators. For example, in this passage Peter literally plays the devil's advocate. Even though Peter has just pronounced a God-inspired profession of faith in Jesus—"You are the messiah, the son of the living God"—he now speaks on behalf of the father of lies. We read: "From that time on, Jesus began to show his disciples that he must go to Jerusalem and undergo great suffering at the hands of the elders and chief priests and scribes, and be killed, and on the third day be raised. And Peter took him aside and began to rebuke him, saying, 'God forbid it, Lord! This must never happen to you.' But he turned and said to Peter, 'Get behind me, Satan! You are a stumbling block to me, for you are setting your mind not on divine things but on human things'" (Matthew 16:21–23).

The fundamental temptation Jesus faced centered on his identity as God's son and his mission to be God's suffering servant who would redeem the world. In other words, this temptation had to do with the truth of who he was and the truth of what he was to do—identity and mission. For the tempter, the stakes are high. Notice that the devil does not try to dissuade him from doing what he is to do. Rather, the tempter suggests another, less costly way of doing it. It is an evasion of the truth to spare pain. We are quite vulnerable to this stratagem, which does not block out the truth entirely but bends it in a different direction with the excuse of making things easier, where the truth is effectively transmuted into a falsehood.

At the end of these considerations of deceptions and lies as reme-dies for pain, certain elements of the tempter's craft become clear. The avoidance of pain grabs our attention and makes us quite vulnerable to the evil one's suggestions. The more effective attacks against the truth do not always involve a full frontal assault. A style that is oblique and evasive seems far more effective. In dealing with these prospects for avoiding pain, we find ourselves before the machinations of deception. We find ourselves facing a practiced adversary.

Deception in the Absence of Love

The very last line of Dante's *Divine Comedy* reads: *"l'amor che move il sole e l'altre stelle"*—the love that moves the sun and the other stars. Love is the fundamental energy of creation. Love is creation's sustain-ing force. The cosmos from the most far-flung galaxy to the smallest subatomic particle is suffused with its creator's love. Creation not only means God making something out of nothing, but also God making something out of love. Here is the ultimate truth of all that we en-counter in the created world, including its origin, its sustaining force, its final destiny. It is love.

Love and truth, according to sacred scripture and Christian tra-dition, maintain an intimate and reciprocal bond. Saint Paul writes about the dynamic element of the Christian life, that is, growth and maturation in Christ. He links truth and love and writes:

> We must no longer be children, tossed to and fro and blown about by every wind of doctrine, by people's trick-ery, by their craftiness in deceitful scheming. But speaking the truth in love, we must grow up in every way into him who is the head, into Christ, from whom the whole body, joined and knit together by every ligament with which it is equipped, as each part is working properly, promotes

the body's growth in building itself up in love (Ephesians 4:14–16).

The same link between love and truth is evident in the Johannine writings, especially in the First Letter of John and its exposition of the Christian life. For example, we read: "Little children, let us love, not in word or speech, but in truth and action. And by this we will know that we are from the truth and will reassure our hearts before him whenever our hearts condemn us; for God is greater than our hearts, and he knows everything" (1 John 3:18–20). The relationship of love and truth is then personalized in our faith in Jesus Christ: "God abides in those who confess that Jesus is the Son of God [the confession of truth], and they abide in God. So we have known and believe the love that God has for us" (1 John 4:15–16).

The correlation of love and truth belongs to the essential core of faith. Jesus is the way, the truth, and the life. His coming among us proclaims that "God so loved the world . . ." (John 3:16). And the fundamental truth is: "God is love" (1 John 4:8). The presence of God in Jesus Christ is marked by love and truth. The absence of love and its correlative, truth, is a sign of the presence of the evil one. Where there is an absence of love, there is also a lack of truth: lies and deceptions. The devil moves in the direction of hatred and even murder and, in so doing, leads people into deeper and murkier realms of untruth, deception. So, we read: "We must not be like Cain who was from the evil one and murdered his brother" (1 John 3:12). Jesus elaborates on this very point in a heated dispute he has with those who will not accept his authority: "You are from your father the devil, and you choose to do your father's desires. He was a murderer from the beginning and does not stand in the truth, because there is no truth in him. When he lies, he speaks according to his own nature, for he is a liar and the father of lies" (John 8:44).

We are accustomed to thinking of "the truth" as an objective, detached, even cold reality. This certainly seems to be the ideal for scientific truth, a reality that many would claim is appropriately detached from human subjectivism and certainly from the vagaries of human love. In fact, there is a way in which the truth correctly stands independent and is not shaped by our opinions or feelings. At the same time, the perspective of faith affirms that "truth," whatever that truth might be, detached from love ceases to be truth and becomes an apparent truth or an outright deception.

The full-scale consequences of detaching truth from love become evident, for example, in certain applications of science to human subjects. Think, for example, of Nazi medical experimentation or the infamous Tuskegee syphilis experiments, or in our own day the manipulations of human life in research that employs human embryos as subjects. In these and other instances, the explicit research intention is to advance the truth and human well-being. In fact, the research actually moves in an opposite direction, that of diminishing human life and growth. Science in these instances is not science as such but something in a deceptive guise of science.

If our concern has been to identify the ways that the evil one can operate as a deceptive presence among us, and by that deception move us away from our journey to God, then the disjunction of truth and love is a most notable strategy because of its great subtlety.

Another variation of splitting truth and love in human life and experience has to do with what ostensibly is a very positive value—honesty. If in the name of honesty, I offer you some difficult feedback but do so without any love or concern for you, then I may have shared accurate information but information that is also deceptive, not fully true. This kind of "honest feedback" implies that what I say defines who you are. It implies that your identity, your value, your place in this world can finally be reduced to the focused and narrow reality that I present to you about you. Notice that honesty without love does not claim that this raw data represents the whole you, the whole person. The distortion and the deception operate at another level—of implication. This is what the feedback suggests or implies about you, about the totality of you. In that implication springing from honesty without love, the truth is wanting, and—true to form—the evil one is able to wreak havoc with someone's life.

In reality, what is happening here is a malevolent enactment of an ancient rhetorical figure of speech called "synecdoche," making a part speak for the whole. In the instance of substantive feedback given without love, negative but true information, a part of the reality of the person, assumes the form of the whole person.

Another example of honest communication without love as a deception may help to clarify this subtle but important dynamic. A physician reports back to a patient the results of a biopsy. The news is not good. It is stage-four cancer. Prospects for remission are very slim and for a cure, non-existent. The physician, a specialist in these matters, must routinely communicate this unfortunate message to patients. To cope with the emotional rebound of this devastating information, the physician detaches from the fuller human context and stays with the facts of the disease. Although the physician's decision is understandable, the lack of empathy in these encounters probably indicates that this decision is bad medical practice, because the communication does not attend to the whole person. At another level, there is also a failure of truth in the communication.

That we are mortal, subject to death, is clearly true. Our encounter with a terminal diagnosis, as painful as this might be, only confirms in a dramatic and immediate way the sense of mortality that we have always carried with us in our lives. When we receive word of this diagnosis without loving concern, what looms ahead of us as our full horizon is our mortality, our impending death. That information or truth shapes us and defines who we are. What begins as the honest communication of medical facts then assumes a totalizing function, defining us entirely in terms of our disease. And that definition is not true. It represents a distortion and, even more fundamentally, an untruth.

We are indeed mortals, and we hold that truth more or less consciously as we move through life. Even more significantly, we are *beloved* mortals. The truth of our lives is not just, in the words of the philosopher Martin Heidegger, that we are *Sein zum Tode* (being-toward-death), as true as that is, but that we are also being-from-love and being-toward-love. So, the lack of love in the communication of the facts of our mortality blocks out the full reality of who we are. We are far more than one part or one dimension of our existence, even that most significant dimension of mortality. The full reality is that we are beloved mortals.

In the clinical example that we have considered, the devil's interest is to detach love from a sharing of information or truth. The truth of the diagnosis, then, seems to stand alone, both objective and independent. It is, however, neither the whole truth of our existence nor a practical truth that helps us to live as we ought. Furthermore, the sharing of the diagnosis without love and our understandable reaction to it draw us and even begin to fix us not only in realms of untruth but also of death. This process also belongs to the devil. He is not only the father of lies and master of deceit, he is also the one who has shaped death as cruel and painful. Death can, in one sense, be seen as a natural pattern of life, no more remarkable than the change of the seasons, a peaceful transition from one form of life to another. Death, however, has assumed a sinister and cruel form as a violent and painful break from life because of sin encouraged and promoted by the evil one. For this reason, the Book of Wisdom says: "For God created us for incorruption, and made us in the image of his own eternity but through the devil's envy death entered the world, and those who belong to his company experience it" (2:23–24).

We began our reflections in this section by trying to understand how removing love from truth leads to deception. Clearly, God's plan indicates an integral relationship of truth, love, and life. The inversion of this holy triad belongs to the evil one, who wants us to be immersed in deception, hatred or indifference, and death. Understanding these subtle but effective stratagems of the devil enables us, with God's help, to meet the devil's challenge of deception.

Summary

The devil's work of deception takes many forms: false promises, complicated tangles, deceptive expressiveness, information substituting for truth, deceitful remedies for pain, and loveless communication. When we summarize these daunting and destructive diabolical strategies, we surely want to echo Saint Paul's question: "Who will rescue me?" (see Romans 7:24). Our response to that question shapes the next and even more decisively important set of reflections that center on Jesus Christ.

Jesus Christ, the Truth, Who Came to Testify to the Truth

By no means have we explored the full range of the possibilities of the devil's deceptions. The strategies that we did examine seem formidable enough. In fact, a quite natural reaction to such a daunting adversary is fear. If we stood alone, fear would appropriately be not only an initial reaction but the abiding state of the soul as we faced the evil one and his strategies of deception. In fact, we do not stand alone, and fear does not have the last word.

According to Walter Kasper, the fundamental Christian stance before the reality of the evil one is not fear but hope in his definitive defeat through Christ's victory over sin and death.[3] In fact, in a Christian context, we can never speak of evil or the devil apart from reference to our faith in Jesus Christ, who has conquered the power of evil through his death and resurrection. I would take this a step further and say that we cannot speak of the particular works of the devil without affirming the healing and redeeming work of Jesus Christ, who conquers evil and the evil one not only in general but also in particular manifestations. So, if a primary work of the devil is deception, a work that unfolds in the course of our daily life, then we must acknowledge the conquest of deception by Christ, who is our truth and came to bear witness to the truth. We need to know the particular victory of Christ, our truth, over the devil's deception. This knowledge enables us to rely on the one who is our true hope. After considering our understanding of Jesus Christ as our truth, we will reflect on the specific dimensions of his victory over all forms of deception.

First, we begin with our experience. In a world marked by sin, deception clouds our life. It is aided, abetted, and encouraged by the evil one, who is the father of lies. If deception takes hold of us and our world—we must always remember this—it happens only with our free, human cooperation and assent. So, it is essential that we recognize the victory of Jesus Christ, who is the truth, as the full horizon of our lives and commit ourselves to live in his kingdom, which is a kingdom of truth. Two key passages in John's Gospel help us to understand these realities.

The first passage is taken from the scene of the Last Supper and an interaction that Jesus has with Thomas. In response to Thomas' question, "Lord, we do not know where you are going. How can we know the way?" Jesus says, "I am the way, and the truth, and the life" (see John 14:5–6). In these words, I understand that Jesus affirms his relationship to the truth in several ways. Because he is the truth, the true word of the Father, he teaches or communicates the true revelation of God to others. Because he is the life, he embodies or incarnates the truth in his very person. Because he is the way, he enables or empowers others to live the truth.

Jesus' mission to teach or reveal the truth, to embody it, and to enable it identifies the very center of his purpose in coming among us. The reality of his purpose frames John's Gospel at the beginning in the prologue and then at the end as Jesus stands before Pilate. The prologue in the first chapter of John's Gospel contains perhaps the most majestic verse in the entire Bible: "And the Word became flesh and lived among us, and we have seen his glory, the glory as of a father's only son, full of grace and truth" (1:14). And a short while later the prologue continues: "The law indeed was given through Moses; grace and truth came through Jesus Christ" (1:17). At the end of the Gospel, as he stands before Pilate, Jesus again affirms his purpose or mission in terms of the truth: "You say that I am a king. For this I was born, and for this I came into the world, to testify to the truth. Everyone who belongs to the truth listens to my voice" (18:37).

Jesus identifies himself with the truth, and he defines his mission as a witness or testimony to the truth. Who he is and what he does converge in the truth. This truth reverses and conquers the work of the devil by uncovering and overturning every deception and untruth. This truth of Jesus sets us free and enables God's life to flourish within us.

Now we can explore the particular shape of Christ's victory in truth over the deceptive manipulations of the devil.

Reality Inverted and False Promises Reversed in the Call to Discipleship

The devil, as we saw earlier, inverts reality and makes false promises that are never kept. He makes alluring offers to enter a controlled future with assured outcomes. He also draws people to evil with a promise that it will not be discovered. And if evil is perpetrated, the devil suggests, it is always mitigated. It is never *that* bad.

In contrast, Jesus—and all the Gospels concur in this—from the very beginning of his ministry calls people to follow him. This call summons people to the truth and to claim responsibility for the truth in a clear-headed and realistic way. The call to discipleship reverses the devil's inversion of reality and false promises.

Jesus says: "Follow me and I will make you fish for people" (see Mark 1:17; 2:13). The followers of Jesus quickly realize that the call of Jesus does not emerge from a blissful dream. Luke's Gospel, for example, underscores the cost of the call:

> As they were going along the road, someone said to him,
> "I will follow you wherever you go." And Jesus said to him,
> "Foxes have holes, and birds of the air have nests, but the
> Son of Man has nowhere to lay his head." To another he
> said, "Follow me." But he said, "Lord, first let me go and
> bury my father." But Jesus said to him, "Let the dead bury
> their own dead; but as for you, go and proclaim the king-
> dom of God." (9:57–60)

Later in Luke's Gospel Jesus says: "Whoever comes to me and does
not hate father and mother, wife and children, brothers and sisters,
yes, and even life itself, cannot be my disciple. Whoever does not carry
the cross and follow me cannot be my disciple" (14:26–27).

The contrast between the way of Jesus and the way of the devil
could not be more pronounced. The devil promises a future and implies a controlled and assured set of outcomes. It is all quite clear but,
of course, completely false. Jesus invites people to follow him by way of
surrender into an unknown and precarious future. The only assurance
Jesus offers is that disciples will be with him and will share his destiny
that leads to the cross. And, instead of mitigating the cost of discipleship, Jesus intensifies the demands and raises the stakes. Some of the
most sacred blood and family relationships pale in comparison to the
relationship with Jesus himself. Furthermore, there is no question of
the disciples concealing anything. Everything is transparent or else all
is lost.

> What I say to you in the dark, tell in the light; and what
> you hear whispered, proclaim from the housetops. . . . Ev-
> eryone therefore who acknowledges me before others, I also
> will acknowledge before my Father in heaven; but whoever
> denies me before others, I also will deny before my Father
> in heaven. (Matthew 10:27, 32–33)

Jesus undermines the devil's temptation that arrives as an invitation
to an assured and controlled future by calling his followers to a surrendered, open, trusting, and transparent way of life. Instead of relying

on false promises, the followers of Jesus rely on one true reality, Jesus himself.

Complicated Tangles Undone by the One Necessary Thing

The occlusion of the truth by layering one complexity upon another is an effective strategy of deception employed by the devil. Complexity can assume many forms. It can be a string of facts, a range of emotions, or a set of circumstances. The form does not matter. The effect is what counts. Faced with complexity, we feel that we can never get at the truth, if, indeed, there even is truth underneath the tangle of things. We do not so much feel deceived as frustrated. Still, the fact is that we are deceived, subtly but effectively deceived that we can never arrive at the truth because of the complexity. We feel a distance from the truth, and that truth may of be great importance—for example, truth about the most significant relationships of our lives, about the social and economic realities that shape our world, or about the values that ought to direct our individual and collective investment of time, money, and energy.

Earlier, we noted how Jesus cut through the tangles of deception in his argument with the Sadducees about the resurrection of the dead. Now, we can continue that exploration of Christ, our truth, who moves us beyond apparent complexities to the simple embrace of truth.

A striking example of Jesus cutting through deceptive tangles to get at the simple truth can be found in Luke's Gospel. Jesus heals a crippled woman in a synagogue on the Sabbath. The passage reads:

> Now he was teaching in one of the synagogues on the Sabbath. And just then there appeared a woman with a spirit that had crippled her for eighteen years. She was bent over and was quite unable to stand up straight. When Jesus saw her, he called her over and said, "Woman, you are set free from your ailment." When he laid his hands on her, immediately she stood up straight and began praising God. But

the leader of the synagogue, indignant because Jesus had cured on the Sabbath, kept saying to the crowd, "There are six days on which work ought to be done; come on these days and be cured, and not on the Sabbath day." But the Lord answered him and said, "You hypocrites! Does not each of you on the Sabbath untie his ox or his donkey from the manger, and lead it away to give it water? And ought not this woman, a daughter of Abraham whom Satan has bound for eighteen years, be set free from this bondage on the Sabbath day?" When he said this, all his opponents were put to shame; and the entire crowd was rejoicing at all the wonderful things he was doing. (13:10–17)

Here, the elements of complexity have to do with a religious law (Sabbath rest) that ought to be observed most especially in a holy place (the synagogue) by religiously committed people (those assembled for worship). These elements of complexity are laid on the situation of a crippled, bent-over woman whose fate, it would seem, is to remain in her infirm condition because a cure would not be appropriate in the circumstances. A cure would not be true to the given religious framework. In one stroke, Jesus, the truth, cuts through the complexities that occlude the reality. According to Jesus, *not* to cure her on this holy day in this holy place in the assembly of religiously committed people would be unfaithful and untrue. Those in attendance at the synagogue service make adjustments for Sabbath observance with regard to their animals. And here is a woman who certainly is not an animal. She occupies a high and holy status as a daughter of Abraham and, in truth, deserves that care and attention that her identity merits.

In saying what he said and doing what he did, Jesus stood in a revered prophetic tradition. The prophets spoke God's truth to the situation of his people, who at times had subverted that truth by layering it with religious regulations. A notable synthetic statement of this prophetic stance is drawn from the prophet Micah, who moves from the complexity of religious observances to the single and true observance of a pure and kind heart:

"With what shall I come before the Lord, and bow myself before God on high? Shall I come before him with burnt offerings, with calves a year old? Will the Lord be pleased with thousands of rams, with ten thousands of rivers of oil? Shall I give my firstborn for my transgression, the fruit of my body for the sin of my soul?" He has told you, O mortal, what is good; and what does the Lord require of you but to do justice, and to love kindness, and to walk humbly with your God? (6:6–8)

Prophetic truth is God's word spoken to particular situations, a given historical moment that needs guidance and direction. In general, prophetic truth means a reorientation or refocusing on the essential reality of people's relationship with God. Micah's words as well as those of Jesus verify this description. Both Micah and Jesus in very different circumstances converge in their proclamation of a single, essential truth that threatens to be obscured by layers of a complexity constituted by poorly understood religious law, its inconsistent application, or its use to evade real responsibilities.

The importance of a penetrating and unitary vision of God's truth finds an illustration in two other passages that belong uniquely to Luke's Gospel. In the first passage, Jesus visits the home of Martha and Mary. Martha is preoccupied with the many details of hospitality, while her sister Mary stays at the feet of Jesus, listening to his words. Martha complains that her sister does not help her. Jesus says: "Martha, Martha, you are worried and distracted by many things; there is need of only one thing. Mary has chosen the better part, which will not be taken away from her" (10:41–42). The sentence "There is need of only one thing" is rendered in the Latin of the Vulgate as the *unum necessarium*, the one necessary thing. That idea has captured an enduring and essential aspect of Christian spirituality for two thousand years. The phrase also expresses the counterpoint to the complex tangle of things that the evil one employs to occlude the truth.

The second passage from Luke is a single but pivotal verse in the Gospel: "When the days drew near for him to be taken up, he set his face to go to Jerusalem" (9:51). This verse marks the beginning of Jesus' journey to Jerusalem, which occupies the remainder of the Gospel. In Jerusalem, he will suffer, die, and rise. After his death and resurrection, the Holy Spirit will come upon the apostles in Jerusalem. Then the holy city will be the point of departure for the message of Jesus Christ to go to the ends of the earth. This single verse that launches Jesus' journey to Jerusalem gives direction to the unfolding of the whole drama of our salvation. In this context, notice not the words of Jesus—there are none—but rather his stance: "he set his face to go to Jerusalem." These words indicate a singularity of focus and purpose, a determination to accomplish the mission entrusted to him. In the complex weave of needs and circumstances, Jesus keeps a unified and unifying mission that breaks through any complexity that would obscure his true purpose. The devil deceives by adding complexity to complexity. Jesus reveals and lives the truth by holding fast to his single, divine purpose.

Paul echoes the simplicity and directness of truth in Jesus Christ. When Paul writes to the Corinthians and speaks of a shift in plans, he anticipates a criticism that he vacillates. In the context of his self-defense, Paul affirms that he takes his pattern for behavior from the singular and simple truth in Christ Jesus. He writes:

> Do I make my plans according to ordinary human standards, ready to say, "Yes, yes" and "No, no" at the same time? As surely as God is faithful, our word to you has not been "Yes and No." For the Son of God, Jesus Christ, whom we proclaimed among you, Silvanus and Timothy and I, was not "Yes and No"; but in him it is always "Yes." For in him every one of God's promises is a "Yes." For this reason it is through him that we say the "Amen," to the glory of God. (2 Corinthians 1:17–20)

In his Sermon on the Mount in Matthew's Gospel, Jesus tells his followers to forego swearing oaths. He summons people to a simple and direct declaration of the truth. At the same time, he suggests that additional flourishes and complications stem from the evil one. Jesus says: "Let your word be 'Yes, Yes' or 'No, No'; anything more than this comes from the evil one" (5:37).

In Jesus Christ, whose glory is "full of grace and truth" (John 1:14), we come to know the victory of truth over the complicating and deceiving entanglements of the evil one. We see and experience truth in its simplicity and directness. We recognize ourselves as summoned to live and to speak in the same way.

Deceptive Expressiveness and True Revelation

A mode of expression, even a very dramatic or intense one, does not guarantee a disclosure of truth. We saw this in the case of religion, sex, and politics—all of which can be in the employ of the devil for his purposes of deception. The devil's confusion of expressiveness with truthfulness demonstrates a masterful subtlety. All too often, we give the currency of truth to something that is said frequently enough, loud enough, and colorfully enough, even though we should know better.

Jesus Christ brings us the victory of truth by being the true revelation of divine truth, the one in whom the mode of communication and the content of the communication correspond entirely. In all that he is and does and says, he reveals God's truth among us. In multiple passages in John's Gospel, Jesus speaks about the truth of his revelation and his fidelity in revealing what he has heard from the Father. For example, in response to Philip at the Last Supper, Jesus says:

> Whoever has seen me has seen the Father. How can you say, "Show us the Father"? Do you not believe that I am in the Father and the Father is in me? The words that I say to you I do not speak on my own; but the Father who dwells in me does his works. Believe me that I am in the Father and the Father is in me. (14:9–11b)

These words of Jesus find an echo in that most Johannine-like passage of Matthew's Gospel: "No one knows the Son except the Father, and no one knows the Father except the Son and anyone to whom the Son chooses to reveal him" (11:27).

A majestic description of Jesus' completely faithful and utterly true revelation of the Father begins the Letter to the Hebrews:

> Long ago God spoke to our ancestors in many and various ways by the prophets, but in these last days he has spoken to us by a Son, whom he appointed heir of all things, through whom he also created the worlds. He is the reflection of God's glory and the exact imprint of God's very being, and he sustains all things by his powerful word. (1:1–3)

These passages from the Scriptures highlight Jesus as the revealer of the truth, the revealer of God. In him and from him, we perceive a transparency, a clear correspondence between his speech and the truth contained in his message. In him, there is no gap, no variance between expressiveness and disclosure. Jesus' revelation or truthful expression constitutes a particular victory over the evil one, who *does* encourage a deceitful variance between expressiveness and honest disclosure, most especially in privileged realms of human expression and relationship— religion, sex, and politics.

The pivotal moment of Jesus' expression or revelation occurs on his cross and in his dying. Although the Scriptures recount a few words that he speaks from the cross, it is the cross itself and his free embrace of it, far more than any particular words, that define his expression and revelation. The language of the cross contains no flourishes and no powerful rhetoric. Rather, the cross speaks a message of self-abnegation and self-emptying out of love. Precisely because the cross represents an ultimate and costly gift, the very gift of life, the cross speaks transparently of the presence of God's love among us. "But God proves his love for us in that while we still were sinners Christ died for us" (Romans 5:8). Mark's Gospel underscores the transparent message of the cross by citing the words of a pagan Roman who was involved in the very execution process but who also finds himself overwhelmed by the revelation of truth that emanates from the cross: "Now when the centurion, who stood facing him, saw that in this way he breathed his last, he said, 'Truly this man was God's Son!'" (15:39).

When those who proclaim the word and those who believe in the word abide in the cross of Jesus, they are enabled to share the victory of truth over the deceits of the evil one. That is the sense of Paul's reminiscence of his preaching among the Corinthians: "For Jews demand signs and Greeks desire wisdom, but we proclaim Christ crucified, a stumbling block to Jews and foolishness to Gentiles, but to those who are the called, both Jews and Greeks, Christ the power of God and the wisdom of God" (1 Corinthians 1:22–24). Regeneration in Christ through his cross and abiding in him who is truth enable us to share his victory over the deceits of the evil one.

We share in that transparent communication of the cross, which is the clear and unambiguous expression of God's love. So concludes the First Letter of John:

> We know that we are God's children, and that the whole world lies under the power of the evil one. And we know that the Son of God has come and has given us understanding so that we may know him who is true, and we are in him who is true, in his Son Jesus Christ. He is the true God and eternal life. (5:19–20)

Information versus Truth and the Triumph of God's Commitment

Earlier we identified a particularly modern phenomenon of substituting information for truth. Although in itself information can be a useful good and of great benefit, it cannot substitute for truth, the truth that grounds us and gives us purpose and direction. The devil can use the potential confusion or substitution of information for truth to deceive people and pull them away from God, who is truth.

In this deceptive confusion of information for truth, how is Jesus Christ, our truth, victorious? How does he show us a path that moves us away from deceptive tactics of the evil one?

Obviously, the biblical witness does not take into account our contemporary situation of an information-driven society. Still, already in the Scriptures there is a differentiation between information, for example, information about people, their characteristics, in contrast to their truth, the real underpinnings of their existence. The exact point of differentiation between information and truth in the Scriptures is commitment taken in a double sense: God's commitment to us and our commitment to God and one another.

The Book of Deuteronomy is a meditation on God's covenant with the people of Israel, a prayerful reflection on God's choice of this people and, in effect, a discovery of God's commitment to his people. The following passage, for example, speaks of this choice or election:

> For you are a people holy to the Lord your God; the Lord your God has chosen you out of all the peoples of the earth to be his people, his treasured possession. It was not because you were more numerous than any other people that the Lord set his heart on you and chose you—for you were the fewest of all peoples. It was because the Lord loved you and kept the oath that he swore to your ancestors. (7:6–8)

Information about Israelites, characteristics of this people, do not suggest a reason for their election as the chosen people. The truth of this choice stems from God's commitment of love for this people. Loving commitment, in other words, trumps information or data.

An exactly parallel situation occurs in the New Testament when Paul writes to the Corinthians. Here, too, God's choice or call is distinctly not based on favorable information or data about the Corinthians but rather on a mysterious and graced commitment on God's part. Paul writes:

> Consider your own call, brothers and sisters: not many of you were wise by human standards, not many were

> powerful, not many were of noble birth. But God chose
> what is foolish in the world to shame the wise; God chose
> what is weak in the world to shame the strong; God chose
> what is low and despised in the world, things that are not,
> to reduce to nothing things that are, so that no one might
> boast in the presence of God. (1 Corinthians 1:26–29)

The truth of the Corinthians rests in the loving commitment of God. Consistently, this pattern prevails throughout the New Testament, for example, in the case of Levi the tax collector, Zaccheus, and the Samaritan woman at the well.

Information is good and useful within its own range. If we are to move beyond information or not confuse information with truth, then we must employ the lens of God's commitment to our broken humanity. God's commitment in love manifested in Jesus Christ establishes our deepest identity as the beloved of God and so identifies the real truth of our existence. Similarly, in our dealings with one another, if truth is to prevail, then we must recognize and identify each other in light of God's commitment to us in Jesus Christ. The priority of the truth *of* each other, based in God's commitment manifest in Jesus Christ, reaches over and beyond the particularities of information or data *about* each other. This priority also shapes the substance of Paul's thought in Galatians: "As many of you as were baptized into Christ have clothed yourselves with Christ. There is no longer Jew or Greek, there is no longer slave or free, there is no longer male and female; for all of you are one in Christ Jesus" (3:27–28).

Here is the standard for those who want to share in Christ's victory over the deceits of the devil, especially in our contemporary context with its flood of information, its scarcity of truth, and its frequent confusion of the two. The first step is not to accept information or data about ourselves or others as the fundamental truth of our existence. The second step is to identify God's commitment to us and to others, a commitment that confers on us our specific identity as the beloved of God. The final step is to understand the truth of our own being and that of others in light of that identity.

Deception Overturned by the Healing of Suffering

In an earlier section, we noted how deceptions and lies are used as remedies for pain or as a means to avoid pain. The prospect of alleviating pain or avoiding it altogether when linked to strategies of deception makes for a very compelling possibility. In other words, we can be strongly tempted to play with truth if it will get us out of pain or walk us around it. We do not want pain. Even more so, we do not want what pain often ushers in—suffering. We need to consider these terms and their exact meaning to understand how Christ, our truth, is victorious over the deceptions and lies that want to manage pain.

In itself, pain can and often does exercise a positive function in our lives. Pain is a discomfort—more or less intense—that alerts us to trouble. Physical pain—for example, an aching tooth—can signal an infection that needs treatment, or, in the case of muscular pain, that we have pushed ourselves too hard. Emotional pain—for example, the consequence of the break-up of a significant relationship—alerts us to the need to recover some equilibrium in our lives. And there is spiritual pain, a distress that can follow our alienation from God and others. That pain can summon us to repentance.

We do not like pain, because it causes unpleasant feelings or states of the soul. Still, it can exercise a positive function by moving us to attend to what needs care. What we really do not like, however, is the suffering that is often ushered in by pain. Although pain may have an emotional or spiritual dimension, its fundamental and primary manifestation is physical. Suffering, in contrast, may have a connection with physical pain, but its fundamental and primary manifestation is in the human spirit. Suffering is the sense of anguish triggered by a disconnection from meaning or from a relationship. Frequently, suffering begins with pain. When the pain has no meaning, seems to lead nowhere, does not connect with a bigger picture, then suffering—the disconnection from meaning—ensues. And we suffer because, in so many ways, we are constituted by our relationships; when a significant relationship is disrupted or interrupted or simply vanishes away, we sense the anguish of disconnection.

Jesus Christ heals suffering by assuming it himself. As he does so, *in* his suffering, he addresses the anguish caused by a lack of meaning and disconnection. He reveals the truth of suffering's meaning, that is, its positive outcome in the mystery of his death and resurrection. He also reveals the truth of our connection or relationship with him and each other, the connection that sustains us. This healing truth enables us to move beyond the short-term strategy of addressing or avoiding pain by employing lies or deceptions, as we might be prompted or tempted to do by the evil one. Let us consider this in more detail.

There are few explicit references in the Gospels to Jesus as the "suffering servant of God." This servant is a messianic figure who appears in four "servant songs" in the book of the prophet Isaiah. Although the explicit references are few, there are many allusions, especially when Jesus speaks of his mission.[4] Jesus draws on the songs of the servant of God in Isaiah to describe his suffering, its purpose, and its meaning. For example, Jesus says of his mission with an allusion to his death: "For the Son of Man came not to be served but to serve, and to give his life a ransom for many" (Mark 10:45). Jesus' words connect with the end of the fourth servant song:

> The righteous one, my servant, shall make many righteous, and he shall bear their iniquities. Therefore I will allot him a portion with the great, and he shall divide the spoil with the strong; because he poured out himself to death, and was numbered with the transgressors; yet he bore the sin of many, and made intercession for the transgressors. (Isaiah 53:11–12)

The suffering of Jesus, which encompasses pain, has a true redemptive purpose or a true meaning that enables him to be victorious over that suffering and pain. In his triumph over pain and suffering, he brings others with him into that victory.

Another significant dimension of suffering is the anguish that follows disconnection. Again, it may begin in pain, but it ends in real suffering. In John's Gospel, Jesus speaks in anticipation of his suffering and death on the cross. At the same time, he pinpoints his undying connection with his heavenly Father: "When you have lifted up the Son of Man, then you will realize that I am he, and that I do nothing on my own, but I speak these things as the Father instructed me. And the one who sent me is with me; he has not left me alone, for I always do what is pleasing to him" (8:28–29). The sense of presence and connection in the course of suffering finds an echo in the third song of the servant in Isaiah: "The Lord God helps me; therefore I have not been disgraced; therefore I have set my face like flint, and I know that I shall not be put to shame; he who vindicates me is near" (50:7–8a). Jesus heals the disconnection that is both emblematic and causative of suffering. *In* his suffering, he connected in an absolutely intimate and true relationship with his heavenly Father.

Jesus heals suffering by freely entering into it and bringing to it both a true meaningful purpose and a true connection to his Father. In doing so, he undermines the devil's temptation to deception based on the desire to either address pain or to avoid it altogether. In Jesus Christ now, there is no need to use evasive or oblique and deceptive strategies to deal with pain and suffering, because they are overcome in him whose suffering has healed our suffering and pain.

Love Reveals Truth

In his encyclical *Caritas in Veritate*, Benedict XVI has underscored the connection between love and truth.[5] According to the Holy Father, action for justice, peace, and the integral development of humanity finds its roots in love. This love, however, to be authentic, must itself be in relationship to the truth. Our own earlier reflections moved toward the same conclusion but from a different starting point. Unless truth is accompanied by love, which in a sense completes it, distortions can follow, and the truth itself can be twisted to become an "untruth." This happens, as we noted, when scientific knowledge without love is applied to a human situation. Such knowledge or truth cannot authentically address the human situation in any kind of integral way. Without love, truth is either diminished or absent. Without genuine love, it is easy to land in the realm of deception.

How can we keep love and truth together? In the Gospel of John, Jesus presents the possibility of "remaining in him" who is both truth and love. So, he says: "If you continue in my word [literally, remain in my word], you are truly my disciples; and you will know the truth, and the truth will make you free" (8:31–32). Later, at the Last Supper and in parallel fashion, Jesus says: "As the Father has loved me, so I have loved you; abide in my love [literally, remain in my love]" (15:9).

Remaining both in the word of Jesus, which is truth, and in the love of Jesus, which is the very love of God, enables the followers of Jesus to integrate or bring together truth and love. This living synthesis assures them a victory over the deceptive ploys of the devil, who wants to separate the truth from love so that, because of the detachment from love, "the truth" is no longer true.

We can clarify this conclusion with some additional reflections on a strange paradox in the Johannine writings. Notice the negative assessment of the world in the First Letter of John:

> Do not love the world or the things in the world. The love of the Father is not in those who love the world; for all that is in the world—the desires of the flesh, the desire of the eyes, the pride in riches—comes not from the Father but from the world. And the world and its desires are passing away, but those who do the will of God live forever. (2:15–17)

Clearly and unambiguously, this passage dissuades the reader from loving the world because it is not of God. Just as clearly, however, and just as unambiguously, another passage expresses God's own surpassing love of the world: "For God so loved the world that he gave his only Son, so that everyone who believes in him may not perish but may have eternal life" (John 3:16). Laid side by side, these passages seem to indicate a lack of consistency or coherence. In fact, the vision is both consistent and coherent.

The world viewed just in its sinful brokenness, as the First Letter of John describes it, is not something to which we should attach ourselves. It is untrue to its origins in its creator. The words of John 3:16, on the other hand, offer a lens through which this broken and alienated world is to be seen. The lens is the love of God that has seen the redemptive possibilities for this world, which are already being actualized in the mission of the Son. The love of God allows us to perceive the fuller truth of the world as something that is full of redemptive potential.

Our participation in the love of God (remaining in this love, using it as a lens through which we view the world and other people) enables us to grasp the full truth of what we are seeing (remaining in his word, remaining in his truth). Our connection with Jesus the redeemer enables our connection of love and truth. Staying on this path allows us to avoid the subtle machinations of the evil one who, for his own purposes of deception, moves us to split truth from love.

Conclusion

We began this chapter with the title "The Ordinary Work of the Devil: Deception." Recall the verse we cited from John's Gospel: "When he lies, he speaks according to his own nature, for he is a liar and the father of lies" (8:44). A reflection on the work of the "father of lies" demonstrates that his work of deception is both ordinary and extraordinary. It is ordinary in the sense that deception can easily be embedded in daily life. The ordinary moments serve as occasions for false promises or complicated tangles or deceptive expressiveness or information substituting for truth or deceitful remedies for pain or loveless communication. If the evil one wants to move us away from our journey to God, who is truth, he has no need for dramatic effects. He can insinuate himself into the events and interactions of ordinary life. There, he can ply his deceitful trade and pull us away from truth.

Despite the ordinariness of the devil's deceits, his work also has an extraordinary dimension. The subtlety and the stealth that mark his deceptions are extraordinary. He moves subtly and stealthily so that he not only draws us into a deceived way of seeing, understanding, and acting, but does so in a deceitful way that seems entirely unremarkable and often unnoticeable. That, indeed, is an extraordinary coalescence of deceitful content and method.

Although we have identified a number of ways that the evil one can employ his deceptive tactics, we have by no means exhausted all the possibilities. What we have considered, however, ought to alert us to this fundamental work of evil in our lives and in the world. In the end, we should be alert and concerned but also confident and hopeful. We can never speak of the devil or the devil's works without reference to the victory of Jesus Christ over evil in all its forms. And we have done this by reflecting on Jesus Christ as the way, the truth, and the life. In him we find our hope and confidence. In him we also find the appropriate and specific means for addressing the stratagems of deception that we may encounter.

3

The Ordinary Work of the Devil:

Division

He knew what they were thinking, and said to them, "Every kingdom divided against itself becomes a desert, and house falls on house. If Satan also is divided against himself, how will his kingdom stand?" (Luke 11:17–18)

A second and ordinary work of the devil is division. Not surprisingly, the evil one's energies are directed to division and disunity, as he tries at all costs to divide people from God, from each other, and from their very selves. The devil works against the very center of our redemption in Jesus Christ, which is our reconciliation and our sharing in the very unity of the Holy Trinity. On the night before he died, Jesus prayed: "As you, Father, are in me and I am in you, may they also be in us, so that the world may believe that you have sent me. The glory that you have given me I have given them, so that they may be one, as we are one, I in them and you in me, that they may become completely one" (John 17:21–23a). Similarly, the Letter to the Ephesians identifies our redemption in Christ with the grace and gift of unity and reconciliation: "Now in Christ Jesus you who once were far off have been brought near by the blood of Christ. For he is our peace; in his flesh he has made both groups into one and has broken down the dividing wall, that is the hostility between us" (2:13–14). The devil's attempts at dividing us represent the counterpoint to Jesus Christ's triumphal work of healing, unifying, and reconciling.

For us who are on the journey toward the fullness of unity with God and with each other, the unity for which the Lord Jesus prayed at the Last Supper, it is decisive that we know and be alert to ways that the evil one employs in his attempts to undermine Christ's work of unity. We will consider the devil's attempts at dividing and splitting on the various levels of our life—personal, interpersonal, social, and spiritual.

The Divided Self

Sadly, some forms of mental illness cause such internal disruption and division within people that they are severely impeded from normal functioning. Illness can render them unable to do the tasks of ordinary life and unable to connect meaningfully with other people. The pathology from which they suffer leads them to experience themselves as divided or as pulled apart from within. The divided self, in this instance, needs medical and psychotherapeutic help to regain a basic sense of wholeness that will permit basic functioning.

There is, however, another experience of the divided self not specifically tied to illness, an experience that is, in fact, common to all human beings. This universal but little-discussed phenomenon is that of the "me and not-me" experience. We all have this experience but rarely talk about it. Freudian psychoanalytic theory might frame the experience in terms of the interplay of the ego, the id, and the superego. I suggest a simpler framework and invite the reader's introspection to verify my assertions.

All of us—when we step back from our experiences—can recognize different currents in our lives. We can account for our ordinary day-to-day experience. Alongside of that, however, we sometimes notice surprising inclinations within us. Some of these inclinations represent high and even noble aspirations of magnificent dimensions that would propel us into a wonderful future. Other inclinations are coarse, exploitative, and downright wicked. These different currents stream together, and when they do, we have an understandable reaction. We say to ourselves, "This is me," and "That is definitely not me," as we sort through what we have observed and identified within ourselves.

The basic process of maturation summons us as we grow up to piece together the different dimensions of ourselves. We try to be consistent and live with integrity so that wholeness and authenticity mark our lives. We try to cease being a jumble of thoughts, feelings, and inclinations that would lead us in many different (and often not good) directions. More and more, we seek to live with a unified and unifying center, our identity or sense of self. Although this is the process of basic maturation, in one form or another the process continues throughout our life as an ongoing project. We may have passed a basic threshold of wholeness, identity, and consistency, but we never lose the need to move forward and deepen these realities. Until we breathe our last, we still grapple with the "me and not-me" experience. This side of death, we can never say that we are finished products—unified, consistent, and fully integrated. And this perpetually unfinished state of life is a point of great vulnerability that the devil uses for his purposes.

As we struggle with the different aspects of our existence, the "me and not-me," the devil can create waves of discouragement—another major work of the evil one, which we will examine in much greater detail later. It is easy enough to discourage someone who may indeed be caught in an interior struggle to find coherence and unity in the disparate pieces of his or her life. We have all had our moments of discouragement with its accompanying temptation to stop trying.

Here we can begin to see a basic strategy of the devil. As much as he possibly can, he wants to stymie us, halt us, and even paralyze us in our life project of bringing a sense of unity to bear on our existence. Although a general sense of discouragement can be quite effective in tempting us to let go of the task at hand, there are also other means that the evil one can use. He can, for example, make us feel overwhelmed by the task of making some coherent and unified sense of our lives. It begins to feel beyond us, out of reach of our capabilities, so that we might as well give up. Another effective move is to stir up our fear, to make us feel frightened as we look at our shadow side or whatever we would rather not set out in the light of day. Fear can easily make us withdraw. The devil can suggest to us that we compare ourselves to others, usually with the subplot of overestimating the progress of others and underestimating ours, so that we look very bad in comparison. Coming up short in comparison to others can effectively halt us in our tracks. The devil can stir up impatience, so we become so agitated and dissatisfied that we want to stop trying. The devil can short-circuit our journey to a wholeness and unity of life with drugs and various forms of addiction. The addictive cycle thoroughly and effectively absorbs us and puts an honest reckoning of our lives out of reach. Again, the point of all these actions of the evil one is to have us stop the life-long project that belongs to us to bring our life together in some unity and coherence. Why is subverting our process of coming to wholeness or integrity of life so important to the devil?

In a word, the devil's interest is to block our integrity of life as a means of blocking our self-gift. The Gospel tells us that we will find our life when we give it back to the God who gave it to us. "For those who want to save their life will lose it, and those who lose their life for my sake, and for the sake of the gospel, will save it" (Mark 8:35). Jesus himself establishes this pattern of letting go of life, surrendering it, so that it may be found again in its fullness. In John's Gospel he talks about his impending death:

> The hour has come for the Son of Man to be glorified. Very truly, I tell you, unless a grain of wheat falls into the earth and dies, it remains just a single grain; but if it dies, it bears much fruit. Those who love their life lose it, and those who hate their life in this world will keep it for eternal life. Whoever serves me must follow me, and where I am there will my servant be. (12:23–26)

In order to give our lives, we must have them as something to give, that is, with a unity, integrity, and coherence about them. We need to have our lives in our hand to be able to hand them over. The devil tries to halt us or stymie us in the process of bringing the different pieces of our lives together, and so he tries to foreclose the possibility of our surrender or of our self-gift to God.

Obviously, we do not want to be subject to the evil one's actions. We want to be free to carry on our life project of bringing unity, coherence, and integrity to our lives so that we make ourselves an acceptable gift to God, in whom we will find the fullness of life. How, then, do we proceed? What are the means for addressing the challenge that is posed to us by the devil, whose interest is to foster our sense of inner division?

There are spiritual resources that can be of help as we confront the temptations to halt the process of gathering our lives together so that we can surrender them to the Lord. In the first place, to foster a unity of life means engaging in a process of change. Biblically, this corresponds to the call to ongoing conversion, a process of continuous change of mind and heart. This call needs to echo and reverberate within us.

Traditional spiritual practice includes asceticism, the discipline of denying ourselves something in order to be freer and more purified of attachments that cling to us and clutter our lives. Asceticism, or ascetic practice, directs us to inner unity and consistency. Fasting, for example, is an ascetic practice that involves denying ourselves food. When accompanied by prayer, fasting helps us to understand our true dependency on God. It heightens our focused attention to the things that truly matter. It moves us forward toward greater unity, coherence, and consistency.

A regular examination of conscience explores how we have failed to live according to God's will. It also alerts us to the grace of God that is active in shaping our lives. An examination of conscience (sometimes in an Ignatian context called a "consciousness examen"[1]) draws us into a more explicit awareness of the movements, both positive and negative, that mark our lives. That awareness is a first and fundamental step in embracing a more unified and consistent way of living.

Spiritual direction is a dialogue of two believers in which one presents the experiences of prayer, struggle, assurance, fear, and hope-filled aspirations to the other with a view toward identifying how God is moving in his or her life. Again, this resource ought to result in a series of understandings and clarifications that identify our unity of life, our identity in God through Jesus Christ and in the Holy Spirit.

The point of these resources—whether embracing an ongoing conversion of heart, ascetic practice, examinations of conscience, or spiritual direction—is to foster self-knowledge. This self-understanding enables us to piece together in a more unified and coherent whole the various elements of our lives. In the Christian spiritual tradition self-knowledge has always maintained a fundamental position in the process of personal development. Self-knowledge is the key to self-acceptance, which, in turn, is the key to self-gift or surrender to God. For this reason, self-knowledge is always prized and valued on the spiritual journey.

Great saints have been convinced of the absolute necessity of self-knowledge on the path to union with God. Saint Teresa of Avila, for example, said:

> This path of self-knowledge must never be abandoned, nor is there on this journey a soul so much a giant that it has no need to return often to the state of an infant and a suckling. And this should never be forgotten. Perhaps I shall speak of it more often because it is very important. There is no stage of prayer so sublime that it isn't necessary to return often to the beginning. Along this path of prayer, self-knowledge and the thought of one's sins is the bread with which all palates must be fed no matter how delicate they may be; they cannot be sustained without this bread.[2]

Saint Teresa understood with other saints that self-knowledge led to a unity of life that, in turn, enabled total surrender to God. She also understood the devil's interest in blocking our self-knowledge as a way of blocking our gift of self to God. For example, the devil might easily stir up a false humility that feeds a divided sense of self that, in turn, impedes spiritual progress. She writes: "I believe the devil harms people who practice prayer and prevents them from advancing by causing them to misunderstand humility. He makes it appear to us that it's pride to have great desires and want to imitate the saints and long to be martyrs. Then he tells us or causes us to think that since we are sinners the deeds of the saints are for our admiration, not our imitation."[3]

The victory over the divided self is self-knowledge that leads to self-acceptance, which, in turn, leads to self-gift—given to God in loving surrender. The evil one's interest is to maintain our internal divisions and confusions, which disable us from giving back to God what God has given to us, namely, our very selves. With God's help, we stay the course or path of self-knowledge, a life-long commitment and task, that brings us to a sense of our identity in God and a capacity to surrender ourselves into God's hands.

Divisions among Us: The Interpersonal Dimension

Clearly, the experience of division is not limited to the divided self as we have considered it. Even more evidently, divisions exist among us in the interpersonal dimension of our lives. Often we find ourselves divided from one another and, depending on circumstances, with a greater or lesser degree of consequence. This is a sad and sometimes heartbreaking fact of life.

We need not ascribe all the divisions we encounter to the devil. On our own, we are quite capable of breaking away from others and sustaining those divisions. Nevertheless, one of the principal works of the evil one is division, setting people against each other. He can directly push or tempt us to split off from others, or he can exploit the divisions we have created on our own. In either case, the creation or maintenance of interpersonal divisions has a place of high priority in the devil's work. Why is this so?

Recall that the devil's work aims to derail our journey to God. That is the sum and substance of his purpose. It is, therefore, critical to understand how we make our journey to God and what the nature of our destination is. Two passages from the New Testament and two citations from the Second Vatican Council can help us understand the essential importance of unity for our journey to God.

In John's Gospel, on the night before Jesus dies he anticipates his redemptive mission and work in the context of his high priestly prayer (chapter 17). With great insistence, Jesus prays for the unity of his disciples and those who follow them. He says:

> I ask not only on behalf of these, but also on behalf of those who will believe in me through their word, that they may all be one. As you, Father, are in me and I am in you, may they also be in us, so that the world may believe that you have sent me. The glory that you have given me I have given them, so that they may be one, as we are one, I in them and you in me, that they may become completely one, so that the world may know that you have sent me and have loved them even as you have loved me. (17:20–23)

The goal or the destination of the disciples of Jesus is unity among themselves, their oneness. The vision, however, stretches beyond the unity among the disciples themselves, for they are to be drawn into the very unity of God, who is Father, Son, and Holy Spirit. In this prayer of Jesus, we understand that the journey to God ends in sharing in the very unity of God, Father, Son, and Holy Spirit. At the same time, the journey itself is made together, that is, in the unity of the gathered disciples.

Another passage from the Letter to the Ephesians describes both the work of our redemption accomplished in Jesus Christ and the journey to participate in that fullness of salvation as marked by unity and reconciliation. We read:

> But now in Christ Jesus you who once were far off have been brought near by the blood of Christ. For he is our

peace; in his flesh he has made both groups into one and has broken down the dividing wall, that is, the hostility between us. He has abolished the law with its commandments and ordinances, that he might create in himself one new humanity in place of the two, thus making peace, and might reconcile both groups to God in one body through the cross, thus putting to death that hostility through it. So he came and proclaimed peace to you who were far off and peace to those who were near; for through him both of us have access in one Spirit to the Father. (2:13–18)

The redemptive work of Jesus Christ includes our reconciliation and unification in the human family as well as our participation in the very life of God, Father, Son, and Holy Spirit.

Both passages—from John's Gospel and the Letter to the Ephesians—underscore the goal or destination of our journey to God as sharing in the unity of the Holy Trinity. Both passages also affirm how we make this journey—together or in unity.

Two citations from the Second Vatican Council's *Dogmatic Constitution on the Church* (*Lumen Gentium*) present this collective and unified journey to God and participation in the life of God as the context for understanding the Church. We read, for example: "[God] has . . . willed to make men [and women] holy and save them, not as individuals without any bond or link between them, but rather to make them into a people who might acknowledge him and serve him in holiness" (9). The opening of that same constitution says: "the Church, in Christ, is in the nature of sacrament—a sign and instrument, that is, of communion with God and of unity among all men [and women]" (1).

The citations from the New Testament and the Second Vatican Council lead us to a simple but critically important understanding: the destination of our journey is unity in God, and the way that we make the journey is in unity with each other. This understanding of both the destination of the journey and the way of the journey as unity explains why the devil is so committed to fostering division as one of his principal works. What remains for us is to understand the principal forms that divisions and separations among us take and then how, in Christ Jesus and by the power of his Holy Spirit, we can address them.

The devil exploits and uses a variety of situations to cause divisions and separations. For example, the promise of something better can move us away and separate us from those who truly deserve our loyal attachment. The classic instance of a promise of something better is found in the Book of Genesis: "But the serpent said to the woman, 'You will not die; for God knows that when you eat of it your eyes will be opened, and you will be like God, knowing good and evil'" (3:4–5). The promise of something better provokes the division between God and Adam and Eve and, in short order, a division between the couple themselves. The lure of "something better" has a powerful effect and can lead to the painful and devastating divisions and separations that happen in adultery and the abandonment of friends.

Another springboard for separation and division are feelings of anger, resentment, and contempt that we may harbor for other people. The story of Judas provides an example of this process. Judas' betrayal of Jesus, that extraordinary act of separation of master and disciple, does not have a clear explanation in the Gospels. One indication, however, suggests that Judas began to feel anger, resentment, and contempt—all directed at Jesus because of the way he dealt with others. So, when Mary, the sister of Martha and Lazarus, anoints the feet of Jesus with costly perfume, "Judas Iscariot, one of his disciples (the one who was about to betray him), said, 'Why was this perfume not sold for three hundred denarii and the money given to the poor?'" (John 12:4–5). The text suggests that he is rankled and even contemptuous of this lavish but loving gesture. His feelings may have pushed him over the brink and led to the betrayal by which he would separate himself from Jesus and the other disciples. It is not uncommon that when we hold others in contempt or their behavior exasperates us we find ourselves alienated from them and want to push away from them.

Still another feeling can lead straight to separation. It is the powerful feeling of fear. On occasion, we are truly afraid of the connection that we have with others because of the potential consequences that may well rebound on us. A classic example of fear leading to separation is Peter's denial of Jesus in the hour of his Passion. Peter is in a courtyard with a servant girl. "When she saw Peter warming himself, she stared at him and said, 'You also were with Jesus, the man from Nazareth.' But he denied it, saying, 'I do not know or understand what you are talking about'" (Mark 14:67–68). This happens a second time. And then there is the almost violent denial in the third round. "But he [Peter] began to curse, and he swore an oath, 'I do not know this man you are talking about'" (Mark 14:71). This remarkable separation of Peter, one of the closest disciples of Jesus' inner circle, from his master in this decisive hour demonstrates how powerfully fear of consequences can affect us and cause us to separate ourselves even from deeply anchored relationships. Jesus anticipated that the evil one would push Peter precisely at this point of his vulnerability. "Simon, Simon, listen! Satan has demanded to sift all of you like wheat, but I have prayed for you that your own faith may not fail; and you, when once you have turned back, strengthen your brothers" (Luke 22:31–32).

Greed or avarice can hold a tight grip on us, focus in a direction of action, and also divide us from each other. "There may not be enough for you *and* me" is the conclusion. "So, we must separate and find our own fortunes individually" is the action or decision that flows from the conclusion. A variation of this pattern of "not enough for you and me" leading to separation belongs to the story of Abram and his nephew Lot. "Now Lot, who went with Abram, also had flocks and herds and tents, so that the land could not support both of them living together; for their possessions were so great that they could not live together, and there was strife between the herders of Abram's livestock and the herders of Lot's livestock" (Genesis 13:5–7). Appropriately, Lot and Abram belong to the same family, for very often families can find themselves divided because of material possessions. Fierce conflicts can erupt when someone in the family feels that he or she has not received a fair share of an inheritance or something of value held by the family. And these conflicts tend to result in terrible, long-lasting divisions.

Another source of division is negative identification. Human groups can formulate an identity, sometimes a very strong identity, based on what or whom they stand against. The division from others stems from a self- or group-defining process. This kind of negatively based identity can be very powerful, even in larger settings, as we shall see shortly. It guarantees clear lines of division and separation.

This process of negative identification results in factionalism. It was evident in the early Christian community. Paul experienced it in Corinth, and he wrote to the Corinthians to address it:

> For as long as there is jealousy and quarreling among you, are you not of the flesh, and behaving according to human inclinations? For when one says, "I belong to Paul," and another, "I belong to Apollos," are you not merely human? What then is Apollos? What is Paul? Servants through whom you came to believe. . . . For we are God's servants, working together, you are God's field, God's building. (1 Corinthians 3:3–5, 9)

Here, as throughout his First Letter to the Corinthians, Paul helps them to move beyond their apparent, often contrived divisions to their common identity and deeper unity in Christ.

Our reflections have by no means exhausted the sources of inter-personal division. The five that we have identified are the promise of something better, resentment-contempt, fear of connection because of consequences, greed, and a negative assertion of identity. Although more provocations of division could be listed, these amply demonstrate powerful sources of division. The devil then exploits these sources of division for his own purposes, that is, to work against our vocation or calling to be one in God, a people reconciled and in communion with God and one another.

The scriptures, particularly the New Testament, suggest paths of resistance to these forces and facts of division. For example, forgiveness

is a fundamental path of resistance to division. Using a numerical figure of speech, Jesus insists on mutual and unlimited forgiveness as a
hallmark of his community of disciples: "Then Peter came and said to
him, 'Lord, if another member of the church sins against me, how often should I forgive? As many as seven times?' Jesus said to him, 'Not
seven times, but, I tell you, seventy-seven times'" (Matthew 18:21–
22). Jesus himself embodies this spirit of unlimited forgiveness that
breaks down divisions, including the remarkable division between him
and his executioners: "Then Jesus said, 'Father, forgive them; for they
do not know what they are doing'" (Luke 23:34).

Also in Luke's Gospel, Jesus introduces a corollary to the universal
commandment to love one's neighbor by summoning his listeners to
universal compassion. This universal compassion, which breaks down
barriers and overcomes divisions, does not represent a heroic exercise
of virtue. It is a normal expectation of someone, that is to say, everyone
who is called to love one's neighbor. He presents this teaching in the
parable of the Good Samaritan. At the end of this well-known story,
Jesus raises a question and then puts forth his command: "'Which of
these three, do you think, was a neighbor to the man who fell into the
hands of the robbers?' He said, 'The one who showed him mercy.' Jesus
said to him, 'Go and do likewise'" (Luke 10:36–37).

We already noted Paul's appeal to the divided Corinthian community to claim their unifying identity. He returns to that theme in a
powerful way as he speaks of the "one body": "For just as the body is
one and has many members, and all the members of the body, though
many, are one body, so it is with Christ. For in the one Spirit we were
all baptized into one body—Jews or Greeks, slaves or free—and we
were all made to drink of one Spirit" (1 Corinthians 12:12–13). To
claim a unified identity counteracts the factionalism that easily tears a
community apart.

These remedies for division and separation are not exhaustive, but
they are powerful—forgiveness, compassion, reclaiming our identity in
the one body of Christ. They address the divisiveness that can be the

product of the devil's work or the divisiveness that the devil seeks to exploit in order to divert our journey into the life of the one God who is Father, Son, and Holy Spirit.

Divisions among Us in the Larger Dimensions of Life

The devil's work is to split or fracture or divide us within ourselves, in the intrapersonal dimension of life, and to do the same in our relationships with others, in the interpersonal dimension. Beyond these dimensions, the evil one works in larger contexts of life, wielding his power and disrupting what ought to be ordinary human interactions.

The biblical scholar Heinrich Schlier, in his masterful exposition *Powers and Principalities in the New Testament*, describes this larger range of destructive and divisive influence that Satan exercises. Schlier explains Paul's understanding of the work of the "principalities" who use their power to thwart the plan of God. They enter into the very atmosphere of human life and institutions and seek domination, which is ultimately divisive. Schlier writes:

> This domination usually begins in the general spirit of the world, or in the spirit of a particular period, attitude, nation or locality. This spirit, in which the "course of the world" rules, is not just floating about freely. Men inhale it and thus pass it on into their institutions and various conditions. In certain situations it becomes concentrated. Indeed, it is so intense and powerful that no individual can escape it.[4]

The world overall finds itself under assault by the destructive and divisive forces of the evil one. One way to view this is to consider the world of money, the world of power, and the world of status. In each of these worlds, the evil one can try to dominate and divide.

The world of money is a ripe field both for destruction and division. Recent events in the world of finance highlight practices that created havoc in the lives of countless people. In fact, no one has remained unaffected by the economic downturn that was caused by profit-driven speculation in real estate and other sectors. It is one thing to subject this current crisis to economic analysis, which can in its own way provide an explanation for the situation in which we find ourselves. It is another thing to step behind the crisis and understand its spiritual origins. In this more interior and less obvious range, we discover a great paradox. People who have the technical and rational skills to manipulate markets do so driven by an irrational greed, because they could never really use all the money that they would garner through their corrupt activity. It is a case of reason in service of the irrational. This suggests the presence and operation of those powers and principalities of which Schlier writes. They are forces for evil that insinuate themselves into every sector of human life and activity.

If we remain in the interior range of the economic crisis, we can also identify the spiritual impact of this crisis. It fosters, first of all, a significant disconnection of people from institutions of public life that are associated with finances. This disconnection, in turn, fosters another disconnection of people from each other. In a time of want, a survival instinct kicks in, and altruism or even fundamental compassion is eclipsed, perhaps even forgotten.

The current difficulties in the economy mean that even those among us who enjoy comfortable circumstances must navigate their investments carefully. Still, the destruction and divisions of our current state pale in comparison to the larger global economic situation. From a world perspective, we live in greatly divided circumstances. There are narrow bands of affluence and wide swaths of poverty and even destitution. Not only do they stand in contrast to each other, but they exist out of sight of each other. The separation of affluence from poverty causes a division of visibility. Without visible presence to each other, the poor and the well-off seem destined to remain separated and divided from each other. And change, so that mutual visibility could bring a shift in the world situation to a more equitable alignment of material goods, seems unlikely.

It is difficult to determine whether world business leaders are aware of papal social teaching. It would seem safe to say that few of them have heard of and fewer still would have read the recent encyclical letter of Benedict XVI, *On Integral Human Development in Charity and Truth* [*Caritas in Veritate*] (2009). The letter addressed the global economic crisis and the enduring poverty of the world's poorest countries. One might legitimately argue the merits of the Holy Father's analysis of or his prescriptions for the economic crisis and world poverty. Significantly, however, no one can indicate another voice raising the issues in a similar way by identifying both the phenomena and the underlying human and spiritual consequences. In a true sense, his is a lone voice summoning the world to solidarity in understanding and addressing the economic system that brings us together and, simultaneously, drives us apart. The fact that the Holy Father's voice and moral assessment are alone and apart by themselves speaks to the significant presence of evil in our world economic situation. The solitary quality in his moral and spiritual assessment of our economics suggests to me that money is an arena of life under the deep sway of the evil one. The devil's particular interest in maintaining a dominant position and voice in the economic field indicates that it provides a most effective backdrop for his work of division and the derailing of our collective journey to God.

In addition to the world of money, the evil one finds an apt arena in the world of power. In itself, power implies no sinister or evil objective. Power, in its most general sense, is simply energy to accomplish a task or operation. In a world marked by sin and the influence of the evil one, however, power can assume a malevolent form. In this sense, power is the capacity to dominate and direct others according to the will of another or the collective will of others. This power imposes itself and draws a strict line of division between the dominator and the dominated. It is self-serving and has little or no regard for the other. Although this negative and even evil use of power can play its part in interpersonal relationships, we will consider it here on a larger scale— in the course of world events. Here, the powers and the principalities can embed themselves in governmental and military structures with great effect.

The twentieth century serves as a textbook of power in the service of divisive evil. Consider two world wars, numerous regional wars and conflicts, genocides, ethnic cleansings, repressive regimes, colonial exploitation, terrorism, and the singularly destructive ideologies of fascism, nazism, and communism. Listed in this way, these events and movements represent an unimaginable quantity of human misery and suffering. The shock of this agony across a century, however, may obscure the common dynamic that lies beneath it all. Whatever happened in the many different exercises of destructive power in the twentieth century had a common substratum; everything conspired to divide people from each other, nations from nations, regions from regions, ethnic groups from ethnic groups. Everyone wielding this power for domination sought to break the human connections, and often they succeeded.

In the twentieth century, the rawest and the most frightening employment of destructive power—in my estimation—was not connected with an event or any actual damage. It remained on the level of threat. This was the strategy known as "mutually assured destruction" (MAD). The two superpowers were, of course, the United States and the Soviet Union, both armed with nuclear weapons and missiles to deliver them. Both nations engaged in an arms race to acquire the most nuclear warheads and the most capable missiles that would deliver them. The build-up of arsenals was meant to have a deterrent effect. The thinking ran along this line: if you strike us and try to destroy us, you may accomplish your goal; but realize that we will unleash our missiles with their warheads and destroy you. With MAD we have an instance of the potential exercise of destructive power to hold the other potentially destructive force at bay. The extraordinary feature of this exercise of world-level power is to take the capacity to dominate beyond its limited divisive effects, disconnecting and separating people from each other, to the realm of annihilation, the extinction of the other, which is the endpoint of the logical progression of division. At a macro-level, we encounter division unto death. This bears the hallmark of the evil one.

When we recognize this context of struggle and power and the outcome of division unto death, then words from the Letter to the Ephesians make clear and penetrating sense:

> Finally, be strong in the Lord and in the strength of his power. Put on the whole armor of God, so that you may be able to stand against the wiles of the devil. For our struggle is not against enemies of blood and flesh, but against the rulers, against the authorities, against the cosmic powers of this present darkness, against the spiritual forces of evil in the heavenly places. Therefore take up the whole armor of God, so that you may be able to withstand on that evil day, and having done everything, to stand firm. Stand firm therefore, and fasten the belt of truth around your waist, and put on the breastplate of righteousness. As shoes for your feet put on whatever will make you ready to proclaim the gospel of peace. With all of these, take the shield of faith, with which you will be able to quench all the flaming arrows of the evil one. Take the helmet of salvation, and the sword of the Spirit, which is the word of God. (6:10–17)

Another important note on the divisive and destructive use of power on a macro-level involves the invocation of religion to underwrite domination. States or groups seeking to establish their own political order in states have invoked religion as the rationale for their use of power to dominate or create domination in a given political context. Today, the *jihadi* movements of radical and fundamentalist Islam come immediately to mind. A quick survey of history, however, suggests that the *jihadi* movements are by no means original in their invocation of religion as they seek to exercise a domination that both controls others and, at the same time, divides true believers from infidels. The pattern is unfortunately frequent in history. It also represents an unfortunate inversion of religious spirit and so, once again, reveals the hand of the evil one.

Religions are structures, such as institutions, hierarchies, and rituals, which embody faith in divine and transcendent reality. Religious markers that stake off religious identity are in service to the faith of the adherents who belong to a particular religion. What is primarily meant to bind believers to divinity can be inverted evilly to serve primarily as a dividing boundary that marks off non-adherents for subjugation or, worse, destruction. In this way, the evil one makes religion itself an instrument in service to the divisive and destructive domination exercised either by the state or would-be political entities. In contrast, genuine religiosity moves in an entirely different direction. The Letter of James says: "Religion that is pure and undefiled before God, the Father, is this: to care for orphans and widows in their distress, and to keep oneself unstained by the world" (1:27). True religion, whatever form it may take, serves compassion, that is, a connection among people, and not their division, as the devil would have it.

We have considered the world of money and the world of power. What remains is to consider the world of status. All three—money, power, and status—are interconnected but feature a different dimension of the human experience susceptible to the corrupting influence of the devil, who fosters division. The claims of status can be particularly divisive.

Status refers to a process of social alignment that establishes rank among people and, often beyond rank, their relative value. Commonly, social status serves to mark social identity, where I belong in this world. Beyond that relatively neutral use of social status, the status of the higher-up can also be an effective position for the exploitation of the down-below class or caste.

A society with strongly defined social stratification, that is, a clear and significant use of status to determine ranking and value, inevitably cannot sustain a spirit of human solidarity. Indeed, it finds itself subject to unhealthy divisions of superior-inferior, person-of-value versus person-without-value. Again, this kind of social setting offers many possibilities for the evil one's work of division.

There are various factors that can establish or contribute to a world of status, for example, economic well-being or impoverishment, level of education, or ancestry. Two factors, however, contribute in an especially significant way to the establishment of a divisive status ranking and valuing. They are race and gender. Although the category of race defies a clear scientific, philosophical, and objective definition, its social use has often defined to what group people belong and what social rank and value they have. This pattern spans worldwide from the *apartheid* of South Africa to the segregation of the United States and the more pervasive social attitude (with many practical consequences) called racism.

The definition of status and value by way of race has spawned a vast quantity of grief in human history ranging from social slights to structured injustice to outright genocide. The inner dynamic is that of division, people split off from one another, and on a macro-level when race creates status and value. Clearly, the devil's work of division can capitalize on this world of status.

Another arena of status has to do with gender, really, the division of humanity in two and then ranking and valuing on the basis of gender. Almost universally, males have had higher status and perceived higher value, a fact that is readily seen in any number of measurable social factors, such as earnings and income, directive positions in business and government, and dramatically in the tragic patterns of prenatal sex selection where it is practiced. This ascription of status and value on the basis of gender has its own name of sexism. It, too, just as racism, has caused much grief in the course of human history, including foreclosed possibilities for life and development, violence, and even death. Like racism, the inner dynamic of sexism, ranking and valuing on the basis of gender, is division that splits one half of humanity from the other half. Again, in this world of status based on gender, the devil's work of division can make great strides. Indeed, in the biblical account of the first sin, the devil had laid the groundwork for the sin of Adam and Eve, a sin which separated them both from God and from each other. God speaks to Eve and says: "Your desire shall be for your husband, and he shall rule over you" (Genesis 3:16). The original design of creation says nothing about status or domination. When sin enters the world, a world of status is established, and the relationship of man and woman becomes infected with division and domination.

At the macro-level, the evil one uses the worlds of money, power, and status to divide people from each other and from God. The counterpoint in the teaching of Jesus is the renunciation of money, dominating power, and claims to privileged status. In the beatitudes narrated in Matthew's Gospel, Jesus says: "Blessed are the poor in spirit, for theirs is the kingdom of heaven" (5:3). In Luke's version, the teaching is even more pointed: "Blessed are you who are poor, for yours is the kingdom of God" (6:20). In the same Gospel, in many places Jesus instructs his disciples on material goods, wealth, poverty, and renunciation. For example, he says:

> Take care! Be on your guard against all kinds of greed; for one's life does not consist in the abundance of possessions. . . . Do not be afraid, little flock, for it is your Father's good pleasure to give you the kingdom. Sell your possessions, and give alms. Make purses for yourselves that do not wear out, an unfailing treasure in heaven, where no thief comes near and no moth destroys. For where your treasure is, there your heart will be also. (12:15, 32–34)

Jesus addresses the world of power and reverses the world's usual patterns of domination. He calls on his disciples to renounce power as the world practices it. Not only does he teach a different path, he also embodies it as the messiah who serves and suffers and so turns the expectations of a dominating and forceful messiah inside out:

> You know that among the Gentiles those whom they recognize as their rulers lord it over them, and their great ones are tyrants over them. But it is not so among you; but

> whoever wishes to become great among you must be the
> servant, and whoever wishes to be first among you must
> be slave of all. For the Son of Man came not to be served
> but to serve, and to give his life a ransom for many. (Mark
> 10:41–45)

Participation in the kingdom of God, according to Jesus, demands the renunciation of privileged status by becoming like a little child and receiving the kingdom as a child. This startling reversal of the world's standards emerges clearly at various points in the Gospels, for example: "Truly I tell you, unless you change and become like children, you will never enter the kingdom of heaven" (Matthew 18:3); and in Luke's Gospel: "Let the little children come to me, and do not stop them; for it is to such as these that the kingdom of God belongs. Truly I tell you, whoever does not receive the kingdom of God as a little child will never enter it" (18:16–17).

The devil's action of dividing humanity from itself and from God works on the larger levels of life—society, cultures, nations, and even the global level. The devil can utilize the fissures arising from the worlds of money, power, and status for his own purposes, or he can create destructive divisions in these arenas. His purpose is simple and direct—to derail our individual and collective journey to God. He does this by alienating us from each other and from God, fracturing and splitting all the relationships of our lives.

Later, we will consider the reconciling and unifying work of Jesus Christ. For now and in this specific domain of money, power, and status, it is enough for us to identify Jesus' fundamental strategy that counters the devil's work. It is the renunciation of money, dominating power, and privileged status. Furthermore, we must note that Jesus not only teaches renunciation but lives this out both as example and as the enabler of our own renunciation. Jesus' renunciation of wealth: "Jesus Christ . . . though he was rich, yet for your sakes he became poor, so that by his poverty you might become rich" (2 Corinthians 8:9). Jesus' renunciation of dominating power: "For who is greater, the one who is at the table or the one who serves? Is it not the one at the table? But I am among you as one who serves" (Luke 22:27). Jesus' renunciation of privileged status:

> Christ Jesus, who, though he was in the form of God, did not regard equality with God as something to be exploited, but emptied himself, taking the form of a slave, being born in human likeness. And being found in human form, he humbled himself and became obedient to the point of death—even death on a cross. (Philippians 2:6–8)

At this point, we can consider more directly our recourse and remedy for the devil's work of division in the reconciling and healing mission of Jesus Christ.

Christ, Our Peace, Who Makes Us One

The Greek word for devil is *diabolos*, the one who is engaged in the activity of *diaballein*, literally "to throw through," in other words, to split or to divide. A fundamental work of the evil one is to divide us from our very selves, from each other, and ultimately from God. We know this work of the devil from our struggles and some of the forms that they take. We struggle with the divided self, with sundered relationships, and with a world that should be home but often feels alien and split within itself.

The counterpoint to the devil's work of division and our struggle with it is the reconciling work of Jesus Christ that brings unity. The most direct and sustained affirmation of the unifying work of Jesus Christ is found in the Letter to the Ephesians:

> Now in Christ Jesus you who once were far off have been brought near by the blood of Christ. For he is our peace; in his flesh he has made both groups into one and has broken down the dividing wall, that is, the hostility between us. He has abolished the law with its commandments and ordinance, that he might create in himself one new humanity in place of the two, thus making peace, and might reconcile both groups to God in one body through the cross,

> thus putting to death that hostility through it. So he came
> and proclaimed peace to you who were far off and peace
> to those who were near; for through him both of us have
> access in one Spirit to the Father. So then you are no lon-
> ger strangers or aliens, but you are citizens with the saints
> and also members of the household of God, built upon the
> foundation of the apostles and prophets, with Christ Jesus
> himself as the cornerstone. In him the whole structure is
> joined together and grows into a holy temple in the Lord; in
> whom you also are built together spiritually into a dwelling
> place for God. (2:13–22)

Clearly, Christ's definitive victory of peace and reconciliation stands over and against all of Satan's attempts to disrupt and divide the inner spirit of believers, the relationships among those who are part of the household of God, and the very cosmos itself, which has been drawn into Christ's reconciling work. Although Christ's victory is definitive, his followers who remain in the world do not definitively share in this victory. They remain pilgrims who have not yet arrived at their destination. They are subject to the temptations and struggles that the evil one provokes. For this reason, the Letter to the Ephesians exhorts Christians to persevere in the life of unity: "I therefore, the prisoner in the Lord, beg you to lead a life worthy of the calling to which you have been called . . . making every effort to maintain the unity of the Spirit in the bond of peace" (4:1–3). Notice that the Ephesians are "called to the unity of the Spirit [and] the bond of peace." They have not arrived at that blessed state of full unity and complete peace. While they live in this earthly condition, they are subject to struggle and temptation. For that reason, a short while later the letter says: "Put on the whole armor of God, so that you may be able to stand against the wiles of the devil" (6:11).

In light of Christ's definitive victory over Satan's attempts to divide humanity from itself, from the world, and from God, and in light of our own provisional status as pilgrims who aspire to live fully and completely the unity and reconciliation won for us by Christ, we can begin to identify strategies for the struggle. We do indeed struggle with the divided self, with sundered relationships, and with an alienated world. How does the word of God illuminate this struggle and offer us a way to meet the devil's temptations?

Struggles of the Divided Self and Possibilities for Integrity of Life

In our understanding of the divided self, Paul's description of himself in the Letter to the Romans looms large: "I do not understand my own actions. For I do not do what I want, but I do the very thing I hate" (7:15). He comes to understand the problem of division within him and, at the same time, he knows that the resources for resolving that division are not within him. Only the power of Christ can heal this broken, divided, wounded man: "Wretched man that I am! Who will rescue me from this body of death? Thanks be to God through Jesus Christ our Lord!" (7:24–25). Paul's response to the struggle of the divided self remains the fundamental response for all of us: remain in Jesus Christ, who heals our divided hearts and spirits. That fundamental response, however, does not preclude other specific responses that may be helpful in addressing particular situations.

On a number of occasions, the Gospels describe Jesus' conflict with the Pharisees and religious authorities. Following the tradition of the prophets, Jesus decries their hypocrisy, in other words, the variance between their professed faith embodied in external behavior and their inauthentic interior commitments. For example, in Mark's Gospel Jesus calls a group of Pharisees and scribes hypocrites and cites the prophet Isaiah: "This people honors me with their lips, but their hearts are far from me; in vain do they worship me, teaching human precepts as doctrines" (7:6–7; see Isaiah 29:13 [LXX]).[5] Jesus illustrates his conclusion by identifying the variance between the commandment to honor one's parents and the Pharisees' evasion of parental support by consecrating material possessions to God. One can understand Jesus' words as a critique of the religious leadership that he encountered. In our context, his assessment also indicates the religiously divided self, the variance between external adherence to religious regulations, and a shallow and self-serving interior commitment to covenantal faith.

A similar but somewhat different situation holds in the parable of the Pharisee and the tax collector (Luke 18:9–14). The Pharisee boasts before God of his righteousness and his religious practices. The tax collector offers a simple prayer for mercy and acknowledges his own sinfulness. The previous example of the scribes and Pharisees indicated a split between exterior behavior and a self-serving commitment to faith. This situation of the Pharisee in contrast to the tax collector suggests a split between exterior behavior, which supposes dependence on God, and an interior commitment that is entirely self-justifying and suggests no need of God.

This missing piece in both instances is the truth of self in God, a consistent truth that would ground both interior commitment and external behavior. The evil one can foster the divided self by using either self-interest or self-justification as a wedge between external behavior and an interior, rationalized commitment. The pull to inner division can be resisted only in Jesus' word of truth that summons us to authenticity both in matching words with behavior and total dependence on God.

There are two other experiences of the divided self in the Gospels. The first is the story of the rich young man that can be found in much the same form in the three synoptic Gospels (Matthew 19:16–22; Mark 10:17–22; Luke 18:18–23). The young man searches for eternal life. Jesus tells him to observe the commandments. He replies that he has done so but asks if there is anything that he still lacks. Then the crucial moment of the encounter unfolds: "Jesus said to him, 'If you wish to be perfect, go, sell your possessions, and give the money to the poor, and you will have treasure in heaven; then come, follow me.' When the young man heard this word, he went away grieving, for he had many possessions" (Matthew 19:21–22). This powerful encounter indicates the divided self of the rich young man. He is a person of great aspirations, including eternal life itself. At the same time, we detect in him a great fear, a desire not just to hold on to his possessions but to retain what those possessions represent—security. The gap or inner split that he experiences disables him from following Jesus. Instead, the Gospel says, "he went away grieving."

A second and similar example of the divided self can be found in the story of the widow's offering (Mark 12:41–44; Luke 21:1–4). In Luke's version we read:

> He looked up and saw rich people putting their gifts into the treasury; he also saw a poor widow put in two small copper coins. He said, "Truly I tell you, this poor widow has put in more than all of them; for all of them have contributed out of their abundance, but she out of her poverty has put in all she had to live on."

In this case, the rich donors experience the divided self. They aspire to generosity, and, indeed, they offer generous gifts—but not completely generous gifts. The rich donors retain something for themselves for whatever reason, perhaps a feared loss of security. There is a divide between their aspiration to generosity and their reserve in giving their gifts. In contrast, with less means, the poor widow gives something that represents a wholehearted gift—*all she had to live on.*

Both the rich young man and the rich donors suffer a similar kind of interior division within themselves. Unlike the Pharisees and scribes of the previous example, they seem to have a grasp of truth. What they lack is a capacity to risk surrender into the hands of God. They aspire to give and to give of themselves. At the same time, they must retain something for themselves and seem unable to give themselves over to God with complete generosity. In the hands of the devil, this need to hold on or this incapacity to give themselves over entirely serves as a wedge dividing them within themselves and, more significantly, from surrendering wholeheartedly to God. The remedy for this partial generosity is association with the one who was complete and unreserved in his giving, because he came "to give his life as a ransom for the many" (Mark 10:45).

Struggles of Sundered Relationships and Reclaiming Communion

We have already considered in detail how we can be divided from each other. There are many ways that we can be split from one another. We have also noted how the devil's interest is well served by our divisions. In resisting these tugs and pulls away from each other, certain strategies clearly emerge in God's word. The ready disposition to forgive one another over and over again certainly heads the list of resistances to division: "'How often should I forgive? As many as seven times?' Jesus said to [Peter], 'Not seven times, but, I tell you, seventy-seven times'" (Matthew 18:21–22). Just as division can be contagious, in other words, one division leads to another, so too, forgiveness can generate forgiveness: "Forgive, and you will be forgiven; give, and it will be given to you . . . for the measure you give will be the measure you get back" (Luke 6:37–38).

Compassion bridges the divide of Jew and Samaritan in Luke's Gospel (10:25–37). And compassion is what links us as neighbors: "'Which of these three, do you think, was a neighbor to the man who fell into the hands of the robbers?' He said, 'The one who showed him mercy.' Jesus said to him, 'Go and do likewise'" (Luke 10:36–37). Compassion connects strangers in the mysterious but real presence of Jesus Christ: "'Truly I tell you, just as you did it to one of the least of these who are members of my family, you did it to me'" (Matthew 25:40).

By God's grace, maintaining fidelity in marriage is a great sign and response to the struggle to remain in communion: "But from the beginning of creation, 'God made them male and female.' 'For this reason a man shall leave his father and mother and shall be joined to his wife,' and the two shall become one flesh. Therefore what God has joined together, let no one separate" (Mark 10:6–9).

Finally, the reclaiming of our communion in the one body of Christ celebrated and made real in the Eucharist mobilizes us to resist every attempt to divide and separate us: "The bread that we break, is it not a sharing in the body of Christ? Because there is one bread, we who are many are one body, for we all partake of the one bread" (1 Corinthians 10:16–17).

The devil's attempts to divide us from each other and to let old divisions fester find formidable resistance in forgiveness, compassion, fidelity, and sacramental communion. Through these means, we share in Christ's reconciling power, and we join in his mission to bring all things into one under his headship (Ephesians 1:10).

In terms of an overall design for Christian living in unity and to foster the healing of division, the Letter to the Colossians offers this by way of summary:

> As God's chosen ones, holy and beloved, clothe your-
> selves with compassion, kindness, humility, meekness, and
> patience. Bear with one another and, if anyone has a com-
> plaint against another, forgive each other; just as the Lord
> has forgiven you, so you also must forgive. Above all, clothe
> yourselves with love, which binds everything together in
> perfect harmony. And let the peace of Christ rule in your
> hearts, to which indeed you were called in the one body.
> (3:12–15)

A Divided World: Healed and Brought to Wholeness

Earlier we considered how the devil uses the worlds of money, power, and status in his attempts to create massive fissures in this world. The evil one moves well beyond the range of intrapersonal and interperson-al possibilities for division to a much wider and more destructive range. By infiltrating the atmosphere (Ephesians 6:12), he infects structures, institutions, political entities—the very instruments we have for liv-ing and working together. A clear arena for this divisive infection that cuts across economics, politics, and social organization is the culture

of illegal drugs. The sale and use of illegal drugs establishes a culture or
environment that co-opts what ought to be the institutions of public
order with a ferocious corruption. The drug culture then rips into communities, neighborhoods, and families and shreds them with violent
cycles of killings and retribution for killings. Finally, the drug culture
breeds a spirit of hopelessness, a sense that nothing can be done, nothing will be done, and everything will collapse in on itself—a nihilism
that crushes every prospect for the human spirit. The drug culture is
nothing less than the demonic powers in high gear. They seem to have
the last word. In fact, they do not.

Those who have staked their hope in Jesus still live in this world
beset and beleaguered by the hostile forces of the evil one who is so
manifest in the worlds of money, power, and status. We have already
seen that the followers of Jesus are called to some form of renunciation;
that they no longer live with money, power, and status in conformity
with the world's standards. Poverty or poverty of spirit, service, and
humility reorganize the lives of believers, who may still suffer the
onslaughts of a wickedly infected divisive culture. This life of renunciation, which means living in the world but not on the world's terms,
does not imply a pure passivity on the part of those who follow Christ.
In fact, Paul and others encourage Christians to an active engagement
of resistance to the powers of evil, as we find, for example, in the Letter to the Ephesians:

> For our struggle is not against enemies of blood and flesh,
> but against the rulers, against the authorities, against the
> cosmic powers of this present darkness, against the spiritual
> forces of evil in the heavenly places. Therefore take up the
> whole armor of God, so that you may be able to withstand
> on that evil day. (6:12–13)

Believers—it is very important to note—are not alone in the
struggle with the powers and principalities who want to dominate and
divide the world. Their victorious Lord walks with them. The word
of God tells us that even now the sovereignty of Jesus Christ and the

coming of the reign of God are upon us. The Letter to the Colossians affirms the cosmic supremacy of Christ. This affirmation must be taken seriously, not as a pious aspiration but as a statement of a fact unfolding now in the course of history. The fact of Christ's supremacy anchors the hope of those who struggle with the divisive ploys of the evil one who falsely claims the upper hand in this world. In Colossians, we read:

> [Jesus Christ] is the image of the invisible God, the first-born of all creation; for in him all things in heaven and on earth were created, things visible and invisible, whether thrones or dominions or rulers or powers—all things have been created through him and for him. He himself is be-fore all things, and in him all things hold together. He is the head of the body, the church; he is the beginning, the firstborn from the dead, so that he might come to have first place in everything. For in him all the fullness of God was pleased to dwell, and through him God was pleased to rec-oncile to himself all things, whether on earth or in heaven, by making peace through the blood of his cross. (1:15–20)

The Holy Spirit has been poured out into the world. If the forces of division are strong, the Spirit is stronger. The Spirit has begun to trans-form divisions into unity, for example, uniting the disparate languages of the human family into a common idiom of understanding: "And how is it that we hear, each of us, in our own native language?" (Acts 2:8). This infusion of the Holy Spirit into the world is not only meant for individual inspiration and interpersonal harmony—although that is certainly the case—but it extends its power into the very unfolding of the cosmos that had been (and sometimes even today seems to contin-ue) under threat by Satan's siege. That is the point of Paul's meditation on the cosmic effects of the Spirit in his letter to the Romans:

> For the creation waits with eager longing for the revealing of the children of God; for the creation was subjected to futility, not of its own will but by the will of the one who subjected it, in hope that the creation itself will be set free from its bondage to decay and will obtain the freedom of

the glory of the children of God. We know that the whole creation has been groaning in labor pains until now; and not only the creation, but we ourselves who have the first fruits of the Spirit, groan inwardly while we wait for adoption, the redemption of our bodies. (8:19–23)

The defeat of Satan and the assured unity of all creation have begun in the resurrection of Jesus Christ from the dead. The hope of the world hinges on his fundamental victory over the forces of sin and death—including those of the evil one. This is Paul's affirmation when he writes to the Corinthians:

In fact Christ has been raised from the dead, the first fruits of those who have died . . . for as all die in Adam, so all will be made alive in Christ. But each in his own order: Christ the first fruits, then at his coming those who belong to Christ. Then comes the end, when he hands over the kingdom to God the Father, after he has destroyed every ruler and every authority and power. For he must reign until he has put all his enemies under his feet. . . . When all things are subjected to him, then the Son himself will also be subjected to the one who put all things in subjection under him, so that God may be all in all. (1 Corinthians 15: 20, 22–25, 28)

Conclusion: The Devil's Wish and Christ's Prayer

We know the devil's wish, not because he speaks it clearly to us, but because we can observe it in his work. Ultimately, he wants to derail our journey to God. He wishes that we would collapse with him into eternal death and everlasting alienation from God. To accomplish this ultimate aim, along the way he wishes for our division and disarray. He wants division to reign from the most intimate sphere of our intrapersonal life to the disruption of our relationships with each other and, ultimately, to a fractured world and cosmos. The devil's wish is as clear as the multiple ways that he afflicts us and our world with divisions.

In an entirely different order and way, we know Christ's prayer for us and for the world. We have no need to deduce it, because he has spoken his word clearly and explicitly. He has prayed before us: "I ask not only on behalf of these but also on behalf of those who will believe in me through their word, that they may all be one. As you, Father, are in me and I am in you, may they also be in us" (John 17:20–21). Elsewhere he has expressed this prayer and has committed himself to action on behalf of the unity he prays for, even to laying down his life: "And I lay down my life for the sheep. I have other sheep that do not belong to this fold. I must bring them also, and they will listen to my voice. So there will be one flock, one shepherd" (John 10:15b–16).

We know the devil's wish. We know Christ's prayer. And we know that Christ's prayer prevails.

4

The Ordinary Work of the Devil:

Diversion

> When the people saw that Moses delayed to come down from the
> mountain, the people gathered around Aaron, and said to him,
> "Come, make gods for us, who shall go before us; as for this Moses,
> the man who brought us up out of the land of Egypt, we do not
> know what has become of him." Aaron said to them, "Take off the
> gold rings that are on the ears of your wives, your sons, and your
> daughters, and bring them to me." So all the people took off the gold
> rings from their ears, and brought them to Aaron. He took the gold
> from them, formed it in a mold, and cast an image of a calf; and they
> said, "These are your gods, O Israel, who brought you up out of the
> land of Egypt!" When Aaron saw this, he built an altar before it; and
> Aaron made proclamation and said, "Tomorrow shall be a festival to
> the Lord." They rose early the next day, and offered burnt offerings
> and brought sacrifices of well-being; and the people sat down to eat
> and drink, and rose up to revel. The Lord said to Moses, "Go down
> at once! Your people, whom you brought up from the land of Egypt,
> have acted perversely; they have been quick to turn aside from the
> way that I commanded them. (Exodus 32:1–8)

The devil wants to cause us ruin, to share—as we noted earlier—
his own situation of everlasting alienation from God. We have
considered how he works to accomplish this goal by drawing us into
a world of deceit or untruth and by dividing us in many ways. Now, a
third strategy or action emerges in his arsenal: diversion. The devil

diverts us on our journey to God, just as the devil moved the people of Israel who were on a journey of freedom away from the worship of the one true God to the worship of false gods. Idolatry, substituting the product of our own creation for the uncreated God, represents the fundamental form of diversion. There are other forms of diversions, as we shall see. The devil can employ them to great effect in trying to move us off course in our journey to God.

The common goal of the evil one's diversionary tactics is to have us lose our focus and our sense of purpose and direction, really, in effect to move us away from our mission. While deception and division can often take on a dramatic form, diversion often operates quite subtly. It may take us a while to realize that we are, indeed, off course and that we have been off course for a while.

The basic remedy for diversion is our willingness to stay attentive to and focused on what God wants of us and to cling to Jesus, who shows how to stay faithful and how to stay true to our direction. For this reason, the Christian spiritual tradition has given great importance to a consideration of the temptations of Jesus as the Gospels recount them. These temptations represent the devil's attempts at the beginning of the public ministry of Jesus to divert him from his mission and purpose. The devil prompts him to change stones into bread to assuage his great hunger after a fast of forty days in the desert. Were he to have done this, Jesus would have moved off a path of pure self-giving and taken a direction of self-satisfaction. The devil tries to entice Jesus with the false promise of power over all the kingdoms of the earth, if only Jesus will fall down and worship him. Were he to have done this, Jesus would have embraced a path other than the one of unstinting attachment and devotion to his heavenly Father and his Father's will as his loyal son. The devil suggests that Jesus throw himself off the parapet of the Temple in a grandiose gesture that would wow the crowds and establish him spectacularly as the awaited messiah. Were he to have done this, Jesus would have veered away from the path of being a suffering messiah who saves us from sin and death by letting himself be subject to their power and vanquishing them from within.

Clearly, diversion is a major stratagem of the evil one. And just as clearly, Jesus forges a path of resolute determination and attachment to the way of God, a determination and attachment that serves as an example and a source of strength and empowerment for us who are subjected to the devil's diversionary tactics. Now we can consider some of the numerous ways that diversion can be manifest on our spiritual journey to God.

Diversion by Absorption in the Task

At first glance, absorption in the task at hand would seem to be a way of staying on track, that is, a way of maintaining a direction. In fact, absorption in a given task does not mean that we have correctly understood the direction that we are to take. This absorption can block our attention to the larger purpose and direction that we are called to take beyond the current task that claims us so intensely. What keeps us occupied may not be bad, but it may not be what should draw our attention and energy, at least in the way that it does.

A specific example of diversion by absorption in a given task emerges in the well-known Gospel story of Martha and Mary (Luke 10:38–42). Jesus visits their home in Bethany. Martha welcomes Jesus and attends to the details of hospitality, while her sister sits at Jesus' feet and listens to him. Martha finds herself busy and without help from her sister. She complains to Jesus and asks him to intervene by telling Mary to help her. Jesus then responds: "Martha, Martha, you are worried and distracted by many things; there is need of only one thing. Mary has chosen the better part, which will not be taken away from her" (10:41–42).

In the history of Christian spirituality, this passage has drawn considerable attention. Writers have attempted to resolve the question of the relationship between contemplation and action, prayer and work. It is unclear to me that these significant questions can find a resolution in these few verses of the Gospel. What is clear is Jesus' warning to Martha and to us: what occupies us—and occupies our time, attention, and energy—may not be what *ought* to occupy us. In fact, our absorption in a given task may divert us from the path that God wants us to be on. In this case, that path is first to be a listening and learning disciple—the foundation upon which everything else in our lives is built.

The story of Martha illustrates how subtle and how powerful a diversion by way of absorption in a task can be. Notice that Martha is doing a very good thing—serving. There is no question about the moral rectitude of her action, and Jesus makes no judgment about her work. In fact, he accepts her hospitality. Notice, too, that she is accomplishing something of value. Finally, notice there is a comparative edge in the story: Martha feels that she is carrying the weight of the day, while her sister does not share the burden. Doing a good thing that amounts to a real accomplishment and seems to excel over what others are doing makes for a very powerful and absorbing focus. Other things, which may be more important, can easily be eclipsed. And that is what happens in this story. Yet a question remains. How or where can we detect the hand of the evil one in this experience of absorption in the task that precludes a fuller grasp of the mission or purpose entrusted to us?

The devil's work in this subtle process of diversion from the true and better purpose occurs, I believe, in his insistence on the currently absorbing task ("You *absolutely must* do this") along with his discouragement of any critical self-reflection or examination ("You don't have any real time or energy to look at this in a different way"). The power of Jesus' words to Martha resides in a message that breaks through that illusory insistence and calls her to another perspective on her activity and commitment.

Diversion by Way of Disdain

It can happen that we are quite clearly aware of a direction and purpose that is entrusted to us. We know that this is what we are supposed to do or, even more pointedly, what we are obligated to do. At the same time, we are repelled by the thought of moving in this direction and doing what is expected of us. Something hooks us and pulls us away from what ought to be done. The hook fixes us on something negative that we scorn or disdain, perhaps thinking and feeling that this is below us, not worthy of us.

A classic biblical instance of diversion by way of disdain is the story of the prophet Jonah. God entrusts Jonah with a very important mission: "Go at once to Nineveh, that great city, and cry out against it; for their wickedness has come up before me" (Jonah 1:2). God is sending Jonah on a mission to call the Ninevites to repentance. Instead of fulfilling this mission entrusted to him, Jonah "set out to flee to Tarshish from the presence of the Lord" (Jonah 1:3). Eventually, he sets sail, is tossed overboard, swallowed by a fish, and spewed forth on a beach. With these hard lessons behind him, Jonah relents and goes to Nineveh. He fulfills the mission. The Ninevites repent, and God spares them.

What is Jonah's reaction? The Book of Jonah says: "This [repentance of the Ninevites] was very displeasing to Jonah, and he became angry" (4:1). Jonah was intensely unhappy that God had spared the people of Nineveh. Apparently, he held them in deep contempt. He disdained them and scorned them. His disdain was so strong that it diverted him from fulfilling the mission entrusted to him by the Lord. He knew his mission, but his strong negative feelings diverted him from accomplishing it. Jonah's feelings of disdain for the people to whom he was sent may actually have been quite well-founded. The people of Nineveh were indeed caught up, as the narrative indicates, in wickedness and evil ways. Jonah, however, goes beyond the simple disdain or scorning of the Ninevites. His refusal to go to Nineveh to proclaim repentance and the possibility of God's mercy includes a disdain of God, who would be merciful to this hapless people.

Jonah's diversion means that he runs away not only from the people of Nineveh, but he also, as the text indicates, runs away from God:

"Jonah set out to flee to Tarshish from the presence of the Lord" (Jonah 1:3). The story of Jonah tells us that disdain or scorn is a truly powerful force for diversion. We may know our mission or purpose very well, as Jonah knew his, and yet find ourselves repelled by fulfilling it because something makes us disdain the mission or those served by the mission or the very one who sends us in mission. It is that "something" that is the hook that pulls us away or diverts us. That "something" poisons the whole prospect of completing what is asked of us.

The devil's hand in diversion by disdain is, in my estimation, quite clear. Two of the devil's characteristics, noted in the Scriptures, are envy and contempt. The Wisdom of Solomon says: "Through the devil's envy death entered the world." The Book of Job, especially the early chapters, pictures Satan as cynical and contemptuous with regard to good man Job:

> Then Satan answered the Lord, "Does Job fear God for nothing? Have you not put a fence around him and his house and all that he has, on every side? You have blessed the work of his hands, and his possessions have increased in the land. But stretch out your hand now, and touch all that he has, and he will curse you to your face." (1:9–11)

If in Satan there is this unholy combination of envy, cynicism, and contempt, surely he can act out of it and plant seeds of it in others, so that they, too, share in the disdain and scorn of the evil one. Once the seed of disdain is planted, it can make the noblest, God-given mission repulsive, as happened to Jonah.

The strategy of diversion by way of disdain is particularly formidable in a church context. The grandest missions can be stymied by an infectious disdain. And that disdain may be prompted by genuinely negative aspects of church life or of church leadership. It is a blessing that the sixteenth-century excesses of church leadership during the time of Ignatius of Loyola and Teresa of Avila did not hook them in the course of their mission to bring renewal and revitalization to the Church. It could have, because there were legitimate grounds for disdain, but both Ignatius and Teresa stayed on the mission and were not dissuaded; they were not hooked. In this, they walked in the footsteps of Jesus, who quite legitimately could have despised the ones he came to save because of their corruption. Instead, he held fast to his mission. Here is Paul's remarkable testimony to this fact:

> For while we were still weak, at the right time Christ died for the ungodly. Indeed, rarely will anyone die for a righteous person—though perhaps for a good person someone might actually dare to die. But God proves his love for us in that while we still were sinners Christ died for us. (Romans 5:6–8)

The effective remedy to the devil's toxic seeds of disdain that halt and divert us is an overriding love that does what love must do.

Diversion by Way of the Polar Opposite

A diversion may mean a slight shifting off course. Of course, even a slight shift can, over time, lead to a serious deviation from the initial path. There are other diversions that operate not by introducing slight deviations but by spinning the affected person around and moving him or her in an entirely different direction.

The common pattern for this kind of diversion begins with a clear and noble purpose or sense of mission. The temptation or enticement is to move in a very different, even opposite direction. If that happens, the original vision becomes corrupted and, ultimately, turned in on itself. If there is recovery from this temptation, there can be a clearer and more determined direction taken. We can consider two classic examples of diversion by way of the polar opposite—for King David and for Saint Anthony of the Desert. Both deal with various temptations, including a strong temptation to lust, but each has a much different outcome.

David sends his soldiers out to do battle while he remains in Jerusalem. David is clearly a man with a mission and a purpose to which God has summoned him. At first, he is pulled off course by his own lustful, wandering eye:

> [David] was walking about on the roof of the king's house,
> [and] he saw from the roof a woman bathing; the woman
> was very beautiful. . . . It was reported, "This is Bathsheba,
> daughter of Eliam, the wife of Uriah the Hittite." So David
> sent messengers to get her, and she came to him, and he lay
> with her. (2 Samuel 11:2–4)

Bathsheba becomes pregnant. David cannot persuade Uriah to disengage from his military commitment to be with his wife so that perhaps the adultery and consequent pregnancy can be covered up. David's next step is to eliminate Uriah. He writes to his field commander, Joab: "Set Uriah in the forefront of the hardest fighting, and then draw back from him, so that he may be struck down and die" (2 Samuel 11:15). And so it happens, and Uriah is killed.

In this sad episode, David is diverted from his mission as a king who is supposed to be a moral and military leader. The diversion amounts to a total turn-around of his responsibilities: first, his adulterous affair; then, his cover-up by way of the murder of one of very own officers and, worse still, using other officers to effectively ambush one of their own. David debases himself and his office by embracing the polar opposite of his mission. Eventually, with the help of the prophet Nathan, David recognizes his sin. He repents and finds forgiveness from God. He is challenged and changed by the experience.

In another instance, the temptation to embrace the polar opposite is resisted. This is the story of Saint Anthony of the Desert, written by Saint Athanasius of Alexandria in *The Life of Anthony*. A short time after his parents' death, Anthony, who had inherited enough money from his parents to lead a very comfortable life, heard a Gospel proclaimed in his local church: "If you want to be perfect, go and sell all you have and give the money to the poor—you will have riches in heaven. Then come and follow me" (Matthew 19:21). Eventually, he makes provision for the care of his younger sister and does embrace an ascetic life of prayer and manual labor in complete poverty.

Athanasius describes how the devil tried to divert Anthony in his resolve to follow this new and transformed life in Christ. Notice how in Athanasius' account the diversion is by way of a frontal assault that attempts to turn Anthony around in the exact opposite direction that his spiritual commitments had led him. Athanasius writes in this telling narrative:

> But the devil, who hates and envies what is good, could not endure to see such a resolution in a youth, but endeavored to carry out against him what he had been wont to effect against others. First of all he tried to lead him away from the discipline, whispering to him the remembrance of his wealth, care for his sister, claims of kindred, love of money, love of glory, the various pleasures of the table and the other relaxations of life, and at last the difficulty of virtue and the labor of it; he suggested also the infirmity of the body and the length of the time. In a word he raised in his mind a great dust of debate, wishing to debar him from his settled purpose. But when the enemy saw himself to be too weak for Antony's determination, and that he rather was conquered by the other's firmness, overthrown by his great faith and falling through his constant payers, then at length putting his trust in the weapons which are "in the navel of his belly" and boasting in them—for they are his first snare for the young—he attacked the young man, disturbing him by night and harassing him by day, so that even the onlookers saw the struggle which was going on between them. The one would suggest foul thoughts and the other counter them with prayers: the one fire him with lust the other, as one who seemed to blush, fortify his body with faith, prayers, and fasting. And the devil, unhappy wight, one night even took upon him the shape of a woman and imitated all her acts simply to beguile Antony. But he, his mind filled with Christ and the nobility inspired by Him, and considering the spirituality of the soul, quenched the coal of the other's deceit. Again the enemy suggested the ease of pleasure. But he like a man filled with rage and grief turned his thoughts to the threatened fire and the gnawing worm, and setting these in array against his adversary, passed through the temptation unscathed.[1]

Notice in this rather lengthy citation from Anthony's life that the devil's temptations are strong and dynamic. They seek to divert Anthony from the path of complete dedication to the Lord, which Anthony has embraced. They do so by pressing in the exact opposite direction of his renunciation: riches, anxiety about responsibilities, lust. The strategy of diversion by way of polar opposites employs a clever psychology that maximizes the power of the temptations. On one level, the temptations reflect powerful human inclinations, especially with regard to the security of having material possessions and the gratification of sexual pleasure. On a second level, these temptations have a familiar ring to them. They stir up a certain nostalgia because they represent what was left behind. On a third level, these temptations trigger yet another and perhaps more dangerous temptation to discouragement. The temptations seem to imply that all the renunciations in the world will never rid even the most pious soul of these forces that would pull us off course. With all these levels operative, there is a central and powerful message that the devil communicates: resistance is useless.

Notice Anthony's resolve and, more importantly, his practice. He stays steady in summoning the Christ who has called him, the Christ to whom he has attached himself, the Christ who is his hope. So, Anthony exercises an oblique resistance. He refuses to fight the fight directly. Instead, he attaches himself to the one who alone has the power to free him, to lead him, and to guide him. Presence to Christ seems to be the effective key to resisting diversion by way of the polar opposite.

This temptation, even if not acted upon, can have a devastating impact on the person subjected to it. The power of the temptation derives from its complete reversal of what the person initially seeks, from the discouraging fact that this reversal still feels like a real possibility, and—most significantly—from the sense of utter aloneness that accompanies the temptation. The presence of Christ alleviates the crushing sense of loneliness and isolation in the face of this kind of temptation.

A final example of a temptation to the polar opposite comes to us from the life of Saint Thérèse of Lisieux. It is her trial of faith that takes hold of her in the last year of her life. This young Carmelite had given herself over entirely to a vowed and dedicated life whose foundation was faith. In the last year of her life, that foundation was shaken. She began to experience a temptation that sought to divert her life of faith into unbelief. She writes in her autobiography:

> At this time I was enjoying such a living faith, such a clear faith, that the thought of heaven made up all my happiness, and I was unable to believe there were really impious people who had no faith. I believed they were actually speaking against their own inner convictions when they denied the existence of heaven, that beautiful heaven where God Himself wanted to be their Eternal Reward. During those very joyful days of the Easter season, Jesus made me feel that there were really souls who have no faith. . . . He permitted my soul to be invaded by the thickest darkness, and that the thought of heaven, up until then so sweet to me, be no longer anything but the cause of struggle and torment. This trial was to last not a few days or a few weeks; it was not to be extinguished until the hour set by God Himself and this hour has not yet come.[2]

Saint Thérèse's response to this devastating temptation follows the pattern of Saint Anthony. She turns to Jesus and clings to him in an act of surrender, a surrender embodied in the last words that she uttered before she died: "Oh! I love Him! [and] My God, I love you."[3] Before those final moments, a few months prior to her death, she had reflected on her response to the great temptation to diversion that would have led her away from God:

> [Jesus] knows very well that while I do not have the joy of faith, I am trying to carry out its works at least. . . . At each new occasion of combat, when my enemy provokes me, I conduct myself bravely. Knowing it is cowardly to enter into a duel, I turn my back on my adversary without deigning to look him in the face; but I run towards my Jesus. I tell

Him I am ready to shed my blood to the last drop to profess
my faith in the existence of heaven.[4]

The temptation of diversion by way of drawing someone to the
polar opposite of their spiritual commitment offers a simple but telling commentary on the spiritual life more generally. No matter the
stage of spiritual life, the depth of commitment, or the apparent solidity in faith, those who follow Jesus are subject to the devil's jarring
and disturbing efforts to move them off of their journey to God. The
resistance and management of this temptation, however, come from a
power infinitely more forceful than the temptation itself: it is the presence of the Lord who accompanies us, the same Lord who was himself
subject to temptation.

Diversion by Way of Distraction

A well-known military strategy to cripple an army's forward movement
is to destroy its communication and command center. If the means of
communication are interrupted and orders cannot be issued, the army
will surely falter. In a similar way, the evil one can divert us on our journey to God by interrupting our communication with God, that is to
say, our prayer. The ordinary interruption of prayer happens because of
distractions, the intrusions that keep us from focusing on our dialogue
with the Lord or our contemplation of his face.

Distractions do not have the dramatic quality of the temptations
to the polar opposite, as we have considered them. They do, however,
erode and divert our relationship with God and our journey to him by
hampering our communication. For communication, after all, is the
mainstay of a relationship and its unfolding.

We will consider four common kinds of distractions that affect our
prayer life and our spiritual life more generally. Before we do so, it may
be good to recall what the *Catechism of the Catholic Church* says about
distractions. One paragraph in the *Catechism* offers a synthesis of the
experience and a response to it. We read:

> The habitual difficulty in prayer is *distraction*. It can affect words and their meaning in vocal prayer; it can concern, more profoundly, him to whom we are praying, in vocal prayer (liturgical or personal), meditation, and contemplative prayer. To set about hunting down distractions would be to fall into their trap, when all that is necessary is to turn back to our heart: for a distraction reveals to us what we are attached to, and this humble awareness before the Lord should awaken our preferential love for him and lead us resolutely to offer him our heart to be purified. Therein lies the battle, the choice of which master to serve. (2729)

Four principal kinds of distractions are anxieties or fears about the future, the slights and offenses that we have suffered at the hands of others, comparisons with the situation of others, and being centered on pleasures of the moment. We will now consider these in greater detail.

In one sense, anxieties and fears about the future are a fixed piece of human nature. They reflect a psychological readiness to anticipate and deal with challenges that will face us in the future. At a certain point, however, they no longer help but hinder our progress. When we find ourselves going in the same circles of worry over and over again without results, we stand in the range of "needless anxiety." When anxieties and fears—whether about the near or remote future—plague our prayer, then they have diverted us from contact with the one in whose providential hands our future rests. In other words, the barrage of worry cuts us off from the God who is our sure source of security.

In his Sermon on the Mount, Jesus speaks to the distraction of anxiety and fear that can have powerful impact on our prayer and our life journey. As he addresses this distraction, notice that he acknowledges it as a reality that we face. In describing the way we fret about our needs and the future, he demonstrates realism about our human condition. Jesus also addresses the remedy for fear and anxiety, which is focus on the providential love of God. We read:

> Therefore I tell you, do not worry about your life, what you
> will eat or what you will drink, or about your body, what
> you will wear. Is not life more than food, and the body more
> than clothing? Look at the birds of the air; they neither sow
> nor reap nor gather into barns, and yet your heavenly Fa-
> ther feeds them. Are you not of more value than they? And
> can any of you by worrying add a single hour to your span
> of life? And why do you worry about clothing? Consider
> the lilies of the field, how they grow; they neither toil nor
> spin, yet I tell you, even Solomon in all his glory was not
> clothed like one of these. But if God so clothes the grass of
> the field, which is alive today and tomorrow is thrown into
> the oven, will he not much more clothe you—you of little
> faith? (Matthew 6:25–30)

Fear and anxiety divert us from our communication with God and
from a sense of forward movement in our journey to God. The same
fear and anxiety—if we follow the words of Jesus—can, in fact, redi-
rect us to the sustaining providence of God. This happens if fear and
anxiety, that is, the preoccupations about our future, remind us of our
reliance on God. Then, what may have been or could have been a
distraction becomes a point of departure for focus on our relationship
with God.

Another distraction that can absorb us and divert us from our relationship with God is the potentially gnawing and constant thought
of slights and offenses that we have suffered at the hands of others. To
be offended, disrespected, and even to be betrayed by others weighs on
us. If for whatever reason we cannot resolve the offense, it can fester
and return at odd moments. The feelings of anger and resentment that
accompany the thought of past offenses easily invade a time of prayer
and communication with God. Prayer is, after all, a time of vulnerability, when we open ourselves to God. That sense of vulnerability
can easily refer us to other moments when we were not only vulnerable but actually wounded. How can we verify this dynamic? It is quite
evident in many of the Psalms. In a particular way, Psalms 52–59 voice

this preoccupation with being offended at the very moment one stands before God in prayer. Consider these verses from Psalm 55:

> Give ear to my prayer, O God, do not hide yourself from my supplication. Attend to me, and answer me; I am troubled in my complaint. I am distraught by the noise of the en-emy, because of the clamor of the wicked. For they bring trouble upon me, and in anger they cherish enmity against me (55:1–3). It is not enemies who taunt me—I could bear that; it is not adversaries who deal insolently with me—I could hide from them. But it is you, my equal, my compan-ion, my familiar friend, with whom I kept pleasant company; we walked in the house of God with the throng (55:12–14). My companion laid hands on a friend and violated a cov-enant with me with speech smoother than butter, but with a heart set on war; with words that were softer than oil, but in fact were drawn swords. (55:20–21)

These ruminations are very distracting and diverting. How do we move beyond the distractions of anger easily awakened by the memory of past offenses and of resentments that have simmered for a long time in an unresolved heart? The very Psalms that voice these preoccu-pations also find resolution in a hope and trust that God will be the ultimate vindicator of wrongs inflicted on us: "But surely, God is my helper; the Lord is the upholder of my life. He will repay my enemies for their evil. In your faithfulness, put an end to them" (54:4–5).

In addition to trust in God as the vindicator of the wrongs inflicted on us, the tradition of prayer—most especially embodied in the Lord's Prayer—includes a petition of forgiveness as a steady refrain. This is forgiveness for ourselves and our failures as well as forgiveness for those who have offended us. "Forgive us our trespasses, as we forgive those who trespass against us." This is also the sense of Jesus' admoni-tion: "So when you are offering your gift at the altar, if you remember that your brother or sister has something against you, leave your gift there before the altar and go; first be reconciled to your brother or sis-ter, and then come and offer your gift" (Matthew 5:23–24). And this pattern of forgiveness as a prelude to the offering of a sacrificial gift finds its culmination in Jesus praying for those who are crucifying him to the cross: "Father, forgive them; for they do not know what they are doing" (Luke 23:34).

Trust in God as the ultimate vindicator of wrongs and the forgiveness of those who have offended us—these are the two remedies that break the spell of a distracting and diverting resentment. We can easily be held hostage by feelings of being slighted and offended. Even more significantly, these feelings can block our communication with God and divert us in our relationship with him. Recognition that this is the case and a turning to God in trust accompanied by a readiness to forgive those who have offended us loosens the grip of this diverting distraction.

A third kind of diverting distraction is comparing ourselves both as who we are and what we have with others. Comparison-making constitutes a dangerous distraction on our journey to God because we focus less on ourselves and more on others. It is for good reason that the last two of the Ten Commandments are given to us and deal with the question of covetousness or illicitly desiring what belongs to another: "You shall not covet your neighbor's house; you shall not covet your neighbor's wife, or male or female slave, or ox, or donkey, or anything that belongs to your neighbor" (Exodus 20:17). Coveting has its roots in comparing and desiring. Coveting has an infectious side that can invade our thinking and feeling and shape our patterns of behavior. In that sense, it can be a dangerous diversion.

Another kind of comparing, and this time in the context of prayer, is evident in Luke's Gospel in the parable of the Pharisee and the tax collector. As the Pharisee approaches God and stands before him in prayer before the temple and alongside a tax collector, the Pharisee says in a high comparative mode: "God, I thank you that I am not like other people: thieves, rogues, adulterers, or even like this tax collector. I fast twice a week; I give a tenth of all my income" (18:11–12). The paradox of the Pharisee's prayer is that he cannot thank God, because he cannot address God directly. He cannot keep his eyes focused on God, because his eyes are looking sideways as he compares himself with others. So, he is diverted or pulled away from his conversation with God, because his comparative way of thinking always leads him back to himself.

These examples suggest to us that a comparative way of living diverts us from our true journey to God. We cannot move forward on the journey by continuously looking sideways. The devil, however, uses this distracting diversion to keep us off the direct path that leads to God.

A final form of distracting diversion is absorption in the pleasure of the moment. Pleasure and enjoyment are not forbidden in the Christian life. Indeed, there is a joyful overflow of our experience of God and his creation. Consider, for example, the opening words of Psalm 84: "How lovely is your dwelling place, O Lord of hosts! My soul longs, indeed it faints for the courts of the Lord; my heart and my flesh sing for joy to the living God" (84:1–2). Those verses and others like them look out and beyond oneself to the grace that suffuses the world. In this context, the experience of joy and the pleasurable resting in this joy leads us forward in the journey to God. It is not diversion but intensification of commitment and direction.

Absorption in the pleasure of the moment or a sense of enclosed self-satisfaction can divert us on the journey to God by pulling us into ourselves and resting there. We then fail to take hold of the movement beyond ourselves, that is, self-transcendence. In other words, this absorption or self-satisfaction diverts us by locking us inside ourselves.

Two examples from the New Testament and an example from the life of Saint Augustine can help us to understand this unusual diversionary temptation that would divert us not by sending us in a different direction but by containing us within ourselves.

The first example is drawn from Saint Luke's Gospel. It is a story particular to Luke. Jesus speaks: "There was a rich man who was dressed in purple and fine linen and who feasted sumptuously every day. And at his gate lay a poor man named Lazarus, covered with sores, who longed to satisfy his hunger with what fell from the rich man's table" (16:19–21). We are familiar with the rest of the story, which concludes with the reversed destinies of the rich man and Lazarus after death. For now, we should focus on these opening verses of the story. With a few select words, Jesus portrays the rich man as someone who is locked into himself by his absorption in pleasure. The rich man is not cruel or even overtly uncaring about Lazarus. He does not see Lazarus; he does not notice him. The rich man is absorbed in the world of his own satisfactions. He is locked in, and so he is diverted from compassion.

A second example comes to us from Saint Paul's first Letter to the Corinthians. Paul rebukes the Corinthian community for the way in which they celebrate the Eucharist. They have been diverted from their true participation in the Eucharist by absorption in their own interests. He writes:

> When you come together, it is not really to eat the Lord's supper. For when the time comes to eat, each of you goes ahead with your own supper, and one goes hungry and another becomes drunk. What! Do you not have homes to eat and drink in? Or do you show contempt for the church of God and humiliate those who have nothing? (1 Corinthians 11:20–22)

The offending Corinthians are self-absorbed and, therefore, diverted from genuine sharing and their true Eucharistic purpose.

A final example is taken from *The Confessions of Saint Augustine*. This autobiography more than anything represents the story of Augustine's conversion. It also serves as a more general template for the conversion of others who want to follow Christ. The process of Augustine's conversion stretches over some thirty-two years, from his birth until the moment he wholeheartedly embraces Jesus Christ. Before his conversion, Augustine spent his time experimenting with various philosophies, religious movements, career moves, and personal relationships. His experiments were designed to enhance his life. In fact, he was quite absorbed in himself and so never quite reached his targeted happiness. A particularly absorbing dimension of his life was his sexual activity, which he could never imagine giving up. As he began, at least intellectually, to recognize the truth of Christianity and, more specifically, Jesus Christ, he also felt conflicted and unable to move toward the faith that beckoned him. He was absorbed and diverted.

Finally, there was a breakthrough. In a garden, he heard a voice saying, "*Tolle, lege*—Pick up and read." He picked up a copy of Saint Paul's letter to the Romans and his eyes fell on these verses: "Not in riots and drunken parties, not in eroticism and indecencies, not in strife and rivalry, but put on the Lord Jesus Christ and make no provision for the flesh in its lusts."[5] At once, he says, he was freed and able to believe wholeheartedly. He did not have to make provision for the flesh. With God's grace, he had overcome this major diversion in his life that took the form of absorption with himself and in himself.

There is a counterpoint to the evil one's machinations to distract us and move us away from our purpose and mission by absorbing us in whatever. That counterpoint is the movement of kenosis, or self-emptying. Saint Paul has this description in his letter to the Philippians:

> Let the same mind be in you that was in Christ Jesus, who, though he was in the form of God, did not regard equality with God as something to be exploited (or alternately translated, to be clung to), but emptied himself, taking the form of a slave, being born in human likeness. And being found in human form, he humbled himself and became obedient to the point of death—even death on a cross. (2:5–8)

To be of this "same mind" is the key to liberation from the distraction of absorption in oneself and one's own gratification.

In general, we have considered the various distractions that cause us to be diverted whether in our communication with God in prayer or on the journey to God. The devil uses these distractions—of anxieties, fears, resentments, a comparative mindset, and absorption in our own pleasures and willfulness—for his purposes, which always seek to move us away from our destiny in God.

Diversion by Way of Conservatism

The devil can use a common human inclination to stay with what is to divert us on the journey to God. A conservative path would seem to be a safer path, but in fact, it can lead us astray. If we cling to our current situation, we can find ourselves unable to go forward. In various circumstances and at different times, the aversion to embracing what is new or moving in a new set of possibilities keeps from our true mission and purpose that God entrusts to us. Several examples in Sacred Scripture come to mind as well as a perspective from Saint Francis Xavier.

A first example of diversionary conservatism comes from the prophet Jeremiah. In the reign of Jehoiakim, Jeremiah addresses the religious and political establishment. The people stand on the brink of disaster but are unwilling to follow a new path of renewal. Rather, they cling to old verities and rigidly hold on to old symbols, particularly the Temple that they transmute into a talisman guaranteeing them security in the face of impending national disaster.

Jeremiah speaks:

> The word that came to Jeremiah from the Lord: Stand in the gate of the Lord's house, and proclaim there this word, and say, Hear the word of the Lord, all you people of Judah, you that enter these gates to worship the Lord. Thus says the Lord of hosts, the God of Israel: Amend your ways and your doings, and let me dwell with you in this place. Do not trust the deceptive words: "This is the temple of the Lord, the temple of the Lord, the temple of the Lord." For if you truly amend your ways and your doings, if you truly act justly one with another, if you do not oppress the alien, the orphan, and the widow, or shed innocent blood in this place, and if you do not go after other gods to your own hurt, then I will dwell with you in this place, in the land that I gave of old to your ancestors forever and ever. (7:1–7)

As Jeremiah describes the situation of the people, especially as it is embodied in the religious and political leadership, there is a stubborn unwillingness to embark on a path of renewal. The path of renewal is caught in the words "amend your ways"—in other words, "Change what you have been doing. Go in a new and renewed direction." Jeremiah's listeners seem incapable of taking up the responsibility for a new direction, which is the direction set by God through the prophet. Instead, they find themselves diverted from that path and caught in old patterns that effectively immobilize them and pull them off the course of God's plan. They cling to an old security that no longer affords protection.

Jesus also speaks about a diversionary form of conservatism in his parable of the talents. The well-known story begins with a man going on a journey and entrusting three of his servants with a certain sum of money—one five talents, another two, and finally the third one talent. The first two servants make investments with the money and get a good return. The third servant follows a different tack: "The one who had received the one talent went off and dug a hole in the ground and hid his master's money" (Matthew 25:18). Then comes the time for the accounting, when the master returns:

> Then the one who had received the one talent also came forward, saying, "Master, I knew that you were a harsh man, reaping where you did not sow, and gathering where you did not scatter seed; so I was afraid, and I went and hid your talent in the ground. Here you have what is yours." But his master replied, "You wicked and lazy slave! You knew, did you, that I reap where I did not sow, and gather where I did not scatter? Then you ought to have invested my money with the bankers, and on my return I would have received what was my own with interest." (Matthew 25:24–27)

In the story of Jeremiah and the Temple, people opt for a "safer" path by clinging to the old ways, assuring themselves that this is a path to security. They do not move forward because of their attachment to old securities. In the parable of the talents, the third servant makes no movement forward and opts for an ultimately conservative and unproductive decision because of fear: "I was afraid." Whether it is attachment to old securities or fear, the result is the same—a diversionary conservatism that keeps people away from an authentic path and moving forward.

A third form of diversionary conservatism appears in Paul's letter to the Galatians. Those who formed the Church in Galatia were converts from paganism who accepted the Gospel of Jesus Christ. After their conversion, "conservative" converts from Judaism approach them and insist on the necessity of circumcision, that is, observance of Jewish law in addition to faith in Jesus Christ. At this point, the Galatians have fallen under the sway of these so-called Judaizers, who cling tenaciously and rigidly to the traditions that they have inherited, not understanding the new freedom and the all-sufficiency to be found in Jesus Christ and the Holy Spirit. Paul writes to the Galatians:

> Listen! I, Paul, am telling you that if you let yourselves be circumcised, Christ will be of no benefit to you. Once again I testify to every man who lets himself be circumcised that he is obliged to obey the entire law. You who want to be justified by the law have cut yourselves off from Christ; you have fallen away from grace. For through the Spirit, by faith, we eagerly wait for the hope of righteousness. For in Christ Jesus neither circumcision nor uncircumcision counts for anything; the only thing that counts is faith working through love. (5:2–6)

The inflexible holding on to the inherited past, the rituals and laws, and reliance on them obviates the need for Jesus Christ and so empties out the new faith that the Galatians have embraced. Staying fixed in the past, they cannot embrace the new thing—justification and life—that comes to them in Jesus Christ. Again, we encounter a conservatism that diverts believers from their true path in Jesus Christ by the power of his Holy Spirit.

A final example of diversionary conservatism comes to us from a letter of Saint Francis Xavier (d. 1552), the great Jesuit missionary of the Far East. The Office of Readings for the feast of Saint Francis Xavier offers a letter that he writes to Saint Ignatius of Loyola. After describing the multitude of people he has converted and cared for, he writes:

> Many, many people hereabouts are not becoming Christians for one reason only: there is nobody to make them Christians. Again and again I have thought of going round the universities of Europe, especially Paris, and everywhere crying out like a madman, riveting the attention of those with more learning than charity: 'What a tragedy: how many souls are being shut out of heaven and falling into hell, thanks to you!' I wish they would work as hard at this as they do at their books, and so settle their account with God for their learning and the talents entrusted to them.[6]

Academics and academic communities often fancy themselves as the avant-garde of progressive or forward-looking thinking. Francis Xavier comes to an exactly opposite assessment of the academics of Europe of his time. He sees them as caught hidebound in traditional academic patterns that render them conservative in their thinking and immobilized in taking bold and innovative action for the sake of the Gospel. They are, according to Francis Xavier, unwitting accomplices of a conservative mindset that cannot grasp the new world that is opening up in the East. They are utterly diverted from a path that would truly cut new ground.

Diversion would seem to be the result of shifting to other directions. As we have considered it, diversion can also be the result of locking into a pattern that immobilizes us from moving on a path that God offers us. As always, the devil can use a diversionary conservatism to tempt us away from the direction that would bring us to God.

The apostle Paul offers an effective remedy for this diversionary conservatism. Regularly in his writings, he urges his readers to recognize the novelty of their new life in Christ and their corresponding call to embrace fully this new way of life. For example, the Letter to the Ephesians says: "You were taught to put away your former way of life, your old self, corrupt and deluded by its lusts, and to be renewed in the spirit of your minds, and to clothe yourselves with the new self, created according to the likeness of God in true righteousness and holiness" (4:22–24). Then Paul elaborates the specific behavioral changes that are consequences of new life in Christ.

Diversion by Way of Relativism

A diversionary conservatism holds that the only thing that matters is what is in hand or what has been perceived to be the fixed tradition. In an opposite way, a practical relativism holds that everything is on a level playing field and that nothing in particular matters.

We cannot and need not consider the theoretical background and the implications of relativism as a philosophical and practical principle of life and action. Pope Benedict XVI and others have given considerable attention to relativism in its various manifestations. For our purposes, this very contemporary mindset has considerable importance for the diversion of our journey to God.

If there is no stable truth, no grounding, then there is no specific direction that is right or appropriate. The prospects for one's life journey become a jumble of disconnected bits and pieces, lacking all form of coherence. In the end it seems futile to search for, much less commit to, a single right direction that would bring us to God. Clearly, in this framework, the journey is diverted from the onset. In a relativistic framework, there is no such direction. For that reason, relativism is such an apt and effective tool in the hands of the evil one.

Although few people have the philosophical sophistication to analyze and understand relativism, the lack of such a background does not disqualify anyone from practicing it. A more accessible expression of relativism among the less philosophically sophisticated would be this: "Nothing matters. Nothing really makes a difference. Everything ends up being about the same." Relativism expressed in this way is a democratic philosophy of life that is easily assimilated and effortlessly implemented.

In a religious context, relativism either embodies a practical athe-ism or suggests that if God exists, he really does not care about our behavior or choices. A meditation on the wicked in Psalm 10 speaks of practical atheism that enables the wicked to do whatever they want: "For the wicked boast of the desires of their heart, those greedy for gain curse and renounce the Lord. In the pride of their countenance the wicked say, 'God will not seek it out'; all their thoughts are, 'There is no God'" (10:3–4). A little later, the Psalm spells this thought out in a slightly different way:

> Their [the wicked's] eyes stealthily watch for the helpless; they lurk in secret like a lion in its covert; they lurk that they may seize the poor; they seize the poor and drag them off in their net. They stoop, they crouch, and the help-less fall by their might. They think in their heart, "God has forgotten, he has hidden his face, he will never see it." (10:8b–9)

Another version of this religiously relativistic mindset appears in the prophet Isaiah. He raises the question of people who feel that God is not paying attention to what they do: "Why do we fast, but you do not see? Why humble ourselves, but you do not notice?" (58:3). The obvious practical corollary to these questions is to do whatever, because nothing seems to matter in God's sight. In a similar vein, the opening reflections of the Book of Ecclesiastes seem to offer a basis for practical relativism because of the lack of consequence for anything at all in the universe: "Vanity of vanities, says the Teacher, vanity of vani-ties! All is vanity" (1:2).

A fundamental resistance to diversionary relativism finds its source and grounding in Jesus Christ. A conscious and deliberate ori-entation to him provides the stable foundation for our future direction on the journey to God. Take, for example, Jesus' words: "I am the way, and the truth, and the life. No one comes to the Father except through me. If you know me, you will know my Father also. From now on you do know him and have seen him" (John 14:6–7). This passage clearly stakes a claim to stable truth in Jesus and a fixed access to God, again in Jesus Christ. An attachment and orientation to Jesus establishes truth beyond all variables and relative possibilities as a steady compass that resists diversion, if not utter dispersion caused by a relativistic mentality. The Pastoral Epistles take up the theme of staying attached and connected to this truth, especially when it is under siege: "I know the one in whom I have put my trust, and I am sure that he is able to guard until that day what I have entrusted to him. Hold to the standard of sound teaching that you have heard from me, in the faith and love that are in Christ Jesus" (2 Timothy 1:12–13).

Diversion by Way of Addiction

The reality of addiction has been with humanity since the beginning. There is even a hint of it in the proto-history contained in the Book of Genesis: "Noah, a man of the soil, was the first to plant a vineyard. He drank some of the wine and became drunk" (9:20–21). The concept, the understanding, and the language of addiction as such, however, are relatively recent. Some would identify the beginnings of Alcoholics Anonymous in the mid-1930s as the beginning of a modern conceptualization of addictions. Although alcohol addiction or alcoholism received initial attention, other forms of addiction both chemical and behavioral have now become part of a common cultural understanding and language.

Addiction in its various forms involves dimensions of human existence that are physical and psychological. Recovery from addiction also entails, at a most fundamental level, a spiritual dimension. Addiction and recovery from addiction are inextricably linked to one's relationship with God and one's journey to God. That is clear from the first three steps of the Twelve Steps of recovery from Alcoholics

Anonymous, steps that are replicated for other addictions as well.[7]
They are as follows:

- Step one: We admitted we were powerless over alcohol
  —that our lives had become unmanageable.

- Step two: We came to believe that a Power greater
  than ourselves could restore us to sanity.

- Step three: We made a decision to turn our wills and
  our lives over to the care of God as we understood
  him.

The first two steps, which deal with powerlessness and faith or trusting hope, certainly bear a spiritual or religious imprint. The third step of surrender (*turn our wills and our lives over*) is a conscious and free choice that bespeaks worshipful entrustment, a centering in God that follows a "de-centering" on alcohol that had assumed the position of an idolatrous center of life.

The fundamental diversion, as we considered it at the beginning of this section, is idolatry, a substitution of a false god for the real God. The evil one is very interested in fostering idolatry because it serves as an entirely apt and efficient way of diverting people from the path to God. The diversionary dimensions of addiction in any of its forms work by placing at the center of one's life something god-like but not God, something that demands attention, devotion, cultivation, and sacrifice—all to the detriment of everything else in life, including the most sacred relationships of family, friends, and God. The idolatrous process set in motion by addiction leads to its inevitable final phase—death, often physical and always spiritual.

Some examples from the biblical tradition and one from the spiritual tradition can help us to appreciate the significance and the subtlety of the diversionary movement of addiction. Obviously, since the framework for addiction is relatively recent, neither the Bible nor the spiritual tradition yields complete case studies of addiction. These sources offer pictures of persons who, in one way or another, fell under the spell of something that was not God and yet for them became a god. As their journeys unfold, they find themselves diverted. In some instances, they regain their direction and reclaim a right path.

A first example, taken from the Book of Judges, is Samson, a strongman and a hero figure. Samson also has a predilection for Philistine women, something that moves him to a disastrous first marriage, consorting with a prostitute, and ultimately falling in love and falling into ruin because of Delilah. He represents more than someone who likes women. They are foreign women, and his connections with them entail some element of danger. He loses his attachment to his people and concomitantly to his God. He recenters his life on these love interests, especially Delilah. He literally becomes powerless in and because of the relationship. The dynamics of addiction are evident in the narrative, even if they remain implicit. Eventually, he regains his strength, a recovery event that somehow correlates his earnest prayer to his rediscovered one true God: "Lord God, remember me and strengthen me only this once, O God, so that with this one act of revenge I may pay back the Philistines for my two eyes" (Judges 16:28).

Samson is diverted in his purpose to defend the Israelite people and to help claim the land for them. The diversion is accomplished through his absorption/addiction to the women of the enemy. He confronts his loss of strength and of his eyes as well as his loss of purpose or direction. He turns back to a path that leads to God by way of prayer that strengthens him and enables him to resume the mission in the final stages of his life.

Another biblical narrative suggests some addictive patterns that are transformed in a process of recovery and renewal. That is the parable of the prodigal son. Obviously, the story is too brief to link all the elements of addiction to this young man, but there is enough implied in the description to make some reasonable extrapolations. The son first detaches himself from his stable center of family life and his relationship to his father. He takes his part of the inheritance and goes off to a foreign land. The parable continues: "There he squandered his property in dissolute living. When he had spent everything, a severe famine took place throughout that country, and he began to be in need. So he went and hired himself out to one of the citizens of that country, who sent him to his fields to feed the pigs" (Luke 15:14–15). The "dissolute living" that leaves him penniless and hungry suggests what the language of addiction calls "bottoming out." He began to be more and more absorbed in his consumption of goods and women (see Luke 15:30) until his appetites led him into a downward spiral and complete ruin among the pigs. He has been thoroughly diverted from his life direction as a son and as a responsible man.

Like Samson, the prodigal son makes an initial move to recovery by way of a prayer that acknowledges his powerlessness and his dependence on his father: "Father, I have sinned against heaven and before you; I am no longer worthy to be called your son; treat me like one of your hired hands" (Luke 15:18–19). In the case of the prodigal son, the diversion is righted. He returns and finds restoration. One of the significant teachings contained in the parable is the possibility of not only finding forgiveness after failure but of rediscovering a lost direction that enables us to journey to God.

A final example of the diversion of addiction comes to us from the ascetic tradition of the desert fathers and mothers. It is the story of Mother Mary of Egypt.[8] The monk Abba Zosimas encounters Mother Mary in the desert beyond the Jordan, according to the story reported by Saint Saphronius. In their encounter Zosimas begs Mary to tell him how she came to be in the desert to live the ascetic life. Reluctantly, she shares her story that begins with her young life and a major turn away from family and home and what can only be termed a thorough attachment to sexual addiction. She describes it in these words:

> My native land, holy father, was Egypt. Already during the lifetime of my parents, when I was twelve years old, I renounced their love and went to Alexandria. I am ashamed to recall how, while there, I at first ruined my maidenhood and then unrestrainedly and insatiably gave myself up to

sensuality. It is more becoming to speak of this briefly, so
that you may just know my passion and lechery; for about
seventeen years, forgive me, I lived like that. I was like a
fire of public debauch. And it was not for the sake of gain—
here I speak the truth. Often when they wished to pay me,
I refused the money. I acted in this way so as to make as
many as possible to try to obtain me, doing free of charge
what gave me pleasure. Do not think that I was rich and
that was the reason why I did not take money. I lived by
begging, often by spinning flax, but I had an insatiable desire and an irrepressible passion for lying in filth. This was
life to me. Every kind of abuse of nature I regarded as life.

She joins a group of pilgrims going to Jerusalem to celebrate
the exaltation of the Holy Cross. On the boat that takes her to Jerusalem, she continues to be immersed in her sexual addiction. The
turning point of her life comes when she is utterly powerless to enter
the church with the other pilgrims. She stands before an icon of the
Blessed Virgin and prays for strength and renounces her profligate life.
At that point she is able to enter the church, and she surrenders her
life to God. She begins life anew. She goes to the desert for forty-seven
years. There Abba Zosimas finds her utterly transformed and drawing him, through her experience, into an understanding of repentance
that he had never had.

Mother Mary of Egypt is aware that her story is not only about
her own sensuality but that the devil has utilized that sensuality to divert her from God. At one point, she prays: "May God defend us from
the evil one and from his designs, for fierce is his struggle against us."
Her story contains all the elements of addiction: detachment from a
healthy life, fixation and absorption on the addiction itself, and a collapse into powerlessness. At the threshold of the church of the Holy
Cross in Jerusalem, Mary experiences with full force her powerlessness
in her inability to enter the church. This propels her to surrender to
the Blessed Virgin and to God. By grace, she reclaims the direction of
her life as a journey to God.

The devil wants to divert us on our journey to God. The pattern of addiction provides an extraordinarily useful instrument for diversion. Our lives, it seems, need some center of worship or adoration. In other words, every person will have his or her central object of devotion, to whom or to which we will give ourselves over. We are created in the image and likeness of God. We come from God, and we are destined to return to God. If that journey is to move forward in its proper way, our lives must be devoted and centered on the God who is our destiny. Addiction short-circuits the journey by inserting another person or object, other than God, for centering, worship, and devotion. The substitute for God amounts to a false god, and addictions can appropriately be identified with the practice of idolatry. A word of qualification is also in order. Addictions are not entirely "devil-driven" phenomena. For addicted people, there are many physical and psychological predispositions and triggers. What the devil can and does do is exploit the addiction as a part of his larger design to keep us from going to God.

The recovery from an addiction that diverts us from God implies a turning or a conversion. It reflects the process that Saint Paul described when he wrote to the Thessalonians of their spiritual journey: "how you turned to God from idols, to serve a living and true God" (1 Thessalonians 1:9). That, of course, is not just the product of human effort but the work of grace.

Conclusion on Diversion

The image of the spiritual life as a journey or pilgrimage has gained considerable attention and acceptance among those who are serious about their spiritual lives. The dimension of journey or pilgrimage highlights the process dimension of our spiritual life. Furthermore, it underscores the incompleteness of this holy enterprise and that we have not yet arrived at our final destination. It is comforting to know that God's life is unfolding within us. Something is given, and something is yet to come. This is the interplay of identity and holy destiny so evident in the words of the First Letter of John: "Beloved, we are God's children now; what we will be has not yet been revealed. What we do know is this: when he is revealed, we will be like him, for we will see him as he is" (3:2).

The image of journey or pilgrimage also suggests that while we are in motion and have not yet arrived, we will inevitably encounter challenges and difficulties. For that reason, the words and the admonition of the First Letter of Peter call us to a holy realism: "Discipline yourselves, keep alert. Like a roaring lion your adversary the devil prowls around, looking for someone to devour. Resist him, steadfast in your faith" (5:8–9). Along the path of the journey or pilgrimage, all kinds of diversions are possible. We have considered some of them, including absorption in a given task, disdain for the mission or direction entrusted to us, embracing the polar opposite of our purpose, distractions that carry us in a thousand directions other than our central direction, a conservatism that is wary of something new even if God is making things new, a relativism that discounts the importance of any specific direction, and addictions that center us on a false center.

The prospects and possibilities of being diverted from the true path in the course of our journey or pilgrimage to God seem utterly daunting. For every one of us, as we enumerate the many ways that we can be diverted, there are twinges of anxiety if not panic. It is easy to go off track, to lose purpose and direction. Furthermore, the devil works with cunning subtlety to pull us away from our authentic path.

What is the remedy for diversion? To stay on the right path and to hold to the true direction, several practices are of great importance. We must, first of all, regularly exercise a self-critical vigilance. This means not taking our life for granted but often reviewing it in light of the word of God. We must also be actively engaged in the Church as the Body of Christ. As we profess our faith that the Holy Spirit is at work in bringing the Church together and leading the Church, we submit ourselves and our lives to the Church for guidance, affirmation, and—at times—correction. In the end, we want to stay attached to Jesus Christ. The Letter to the Hebrews expresses this preserving attachment to the journey in the company of Jesus this way: "Let us run with perseverance the race that is set before us, looking to Jesus the pioneer and perfecter of our faith, who for the sake of the joy that was set before him endured the cross, disregarding its shame, and has taken his seat at the right hand of the throne of God" (12:1–2).

Although we may feel severely challenged by the prospects of diversion that will inevitably come our way along the journey to God, we cannot claim responsibility for our fidelity. It is not our work. For this reason, the words of Paul in his Letter to the Philippians must find a steady echo in our minds and hearts. The key is identifying the source of confidence not in ourselves but in God. In this line, Paul writes: "I am confident of this, that the one who began a good work among you will bring it to completion by the day of Jesus Christ" (1:6).

5

The Ordinary Work of the Devil:

Discouragement

The devil is not exclusively responsible for discouragement in our world. Other people, wearying life circumstances, and our own sin and limitations—all these and more can breed a depth of discouragement in our lives. The devil, however, adroitly uses discouragement for his own purpose, which is to thwart us on our way to God. It remains a potent weapon in his hands. Discouragement, if pervasive and insistently present to us, can halt us or even paralyze us on the journey to God. Spiritual writers from the time of the desert fathers and mothers have seen discouragement as a most dangerous, if not *the* most dangerous, threat to the spiritual life. Discouragement imperils the entire journey.

Apart from a spiritual or explicitly religious context, discouragement—from my perspective—is pandemic in our society. Everyone seems touched by discouragement. The causes are many, ranging from failed expectations of relationships to work to one's personal future. As a phenomenon, discouragement becomes evident in the listlessness and the tiredness that mark so many people. Discouragement manifests itself on the joyless faces of people who ride a bus, walk a city street, or even sit on the pews of a church on Sunday.

Sometimes, I wonder if depression is diagnosed too often, when, in fact, the real problem is discouragement. I suspect that there may be many more people who are discouraged rather than those who are depressed. The two conditions are different, although the manifestations may often appear to be the same and, at times, long-term and intense discouragement may lead to depression. Severe or acute depression, however, is a crushing sadness that comes upon us because of chemical imbalances or very painful situations, such as the experience of significant loss. There seems to be no way out. Depression's neighbor is despair—the utter forsaking of all hope. "*Lasciate ogni speranza voi ch'entrate. . . .* Abandon all hope ye who enter." Dante's words above the portals of hell ring true to those who have been swept into a deep and dark hole of depression. They have abandoned hope, or, more accurately, hope has abandoned them. And apart from the intense feelings of sadness and a panicky sense of being pulled into a vortex of nothingness, depressed persons find themselves numb to other feelings.

Although they generally feel sad, discouraged people are not necessarily depressed. Unlike the acutely depressed, the discouraged are clearly aware of potential and possibility. Precisely because they know what could be, the thwarting or impeding of the possibility weighs down upon them. They seem to replay the story of Tantalus, the mythic figure who had luscious fruit near him but never quite within reach. The illness of depression makes decisions for those whom it afflicts. It limits their movement, their activity, and their relationships. Discouragement, on the other hand, leads people to make decisions often to stop trying or to pull back or to do something else or simply come to a halt. It is that little edge of freedom to decide in discouragement that is of such great interest to the devil, who knows that the journey to God is all about freedom and that, in the end, all God wants of us is our free and loving response to him.

The devil indeed uses discouragement to damage and even derail our journey to God. This insidious strategy can go unnoticed, in the sense that the devil's hand is not clearly evident nor is the thwarting of the journey away from God apparent. It is quite possible—and to the devil's advantage—to be so caught up in the spirit of discouragement that one does not notice the larger horizon of life.

Discouragement and Acedia

Obviously, discouragement is not the invention of our age and experience. In its general shape, discouragement has been with humanity from the beginning. As we have already noted, discouragement has particular significance for those on the spiritual journey. And the Christian spiritual tradition has addressed it in various ways. Spiritual writers have reflected on acedia, one of the capital sins or major temptations of the Christian life that lead to sin. It will be helpful to explore the concept and the experience of acedia, because it offers access to the domain of spiritual discouragement as a work of the evil one and, eventually, helps us to respond to it.

Acedia comes from the Greek word *akedeo*, which translates as "I do not care." It signifies a kind of indifference or wistful weariness or even a kind of sad resignation. Across the Christian tradition—spiritual, theological, moral, and pastoral—acedia has acquired different nuances.[1] They include a sense of melancholy, listlessness, disdain for the things of God and for the very love of God, sloth or laziness in general, laziness with regard to religious obligations and practices, and—of course—discouragement.

The earliest explorations of the phenomenon of acedia come to us from the tradition of the desert fathers and mothers and early monasticism. These reflections—in my estimation—remain among the most valuable because of their penetrating analyses and practical value. Eventually, spiritual and moral commentators reduce acedia to laziness or sloth, the common expression of the capital sin. If we stay with the earlier commentary on acedia, we can probe with greater precision how the devil uses discouragement to harm us on the spiritual journey.

The first detailed description of acedia comes to us from Evagrius Ponticus (d. 399), a preacher in Constantinople who eventually withdrew and lived among the hermit-monks. He was one of the earliest witnesses of the wisdom of the desert and the first to systematize the capital sins or, more precisely, the capital vices that lead to sin. Here is a detailed description of acedia from Evagrius, which we can later parse for its multiple meanings and implications:

> The demon of **acedia**, also called "noonday demon," is the most oppressive of all demons. He attacks the monk about the fourth hour and besieges his soul until the eighth hour. First he makes the sun appear sluggish and immobile, as if the day had fifty hours. Then he causes the monk continually to look at the windows and forces him to step out of his cell and to gaze at the sun to see how far it still is from the ninth hour, and to look around, here and there, whether any of his brethren is near. Moreover, the demon sends him hatred against the place, against life itself, and against the work of his hands, and makes him think he has lost the love among his brethren and that there is none to comfort him. If during those days anybody annoyed the monk, the demon would add this to increase the monk's hatred. He stirs the monk also to long for different places in which he can find easily what is necessary for his life and can carry on a much less toilsome and more expedient profession. It is not on account of the locality, the demon suggests, that one pleases God. He can be worshipped everywhere. To these thoughts the demon adds the memory of the monk's family and of his former way of life. He presents the length of his lifetime, holding before the monk's eyes all the hardships of his ascetic life. Thus the demon employs all his wiles so that the monk may leave his cell and flee from the race-course.[2]

Before acedia takes hold of persons—it is important to note—they have made some form of a very good, even noble commitment. The desert fathers and mothers, for example, went to the desert to live out a radical form of discipleship. Through a life dedicated wholeheartedly to prayer and fasting and works of penance, they sought a purified heart that would enable them to grow close to God. Discouragement, as we shall see, does not happen because someone has done something bad or been negligent. On the contrary, discouragement comes with trying to do what is good and, more specifically in our context, trying to embrace the holy.

Notice in Evagrius's description of acedia that he calls it the "noonday demon." This is a reference to Psalm 90:6 of the Vulgate (Saint Jerome's translation of the Bible into Latin), which speaks of God protecting the just person from the incursions of the *daemonium meridianum*, the noonday demon or devil. Even though Jerome's Latin translation of the original Hebrew is found wanting today, the "noonday demon" reference has its own importance in identifying *when* devout believers might encounter acedia as a temptation directed toward them by the evil one.

Acedia happens not at the dawn or beginning of a deliberate and intentional spiritual journey. Acedia belongs as a temptation to those who have been on the journey for a while, that is, at noontime. Evagrius also calls it the most oppressive or most dangerous temptation, because it leads those tempted out of their commitment to abandon their special spiritual journey entirely. So, acedia causes a complete subversion of the journey. The stakes are very high. Acedia can rightly be called the most oppressive and the most dangerous temptation.

In his extensive study of acedia, Siegfried Wenzel notes the many traits, characteristics, and effects of this temptation among the desert fathers and mothers and early monastics. They include psychic exhaustion, listlessness caused by monotony, dejection, restlessness, hatred of one's cell, hatred of one's brethren, and a strong desire to leave and go and do something else. As I consider Evagrius's description of acedia above and reflect on other accounts, I think that discouragement can link together most of the aspects or elements of acedia.

The First Form of Acedia: From Discouragement to Regression

Here is how acedia as discouragement touched the lives and spiritual journeys of the fathers and mothers of the desert who had gone there to live the Christian life of discipleship in a radical form. The noonday devil approached those he tempted in at least three different ways. Remember that the person tempted had to have been on the journey for a while. Then, the demon might first say, "Look, you came out to the desert to be close to God. But look at you. You are no different now than when you first came out here. You might as well go back to the world and your former way of life." This first form of acedia introduces a sense of discouragement by highlighting a lack of spiritual progress. And in the matter of spiritual progress, it must be said, we are very vulnerable. Sometimes the measures for such progress are lacking. There is nothing empirical and quantifiable, something that could be easily measured. Progress in the spiritual life, after all, has to do with the quality of our relationship with God and others, a matter of love. The presence of love leaves signs of compassion and dedication, but it leaves nothing that could be measured.

At other times, through the tricks of memory and imagination, we seem to be back to a time that we thought we had left long ago. This happened to Saint Augustine years after his conversion. When he was a bishop and writing his *Confessions*, the narrative of his spiritual journey, he struggled with his past that seemed to dog him into the present. He spoke with God and wrote:

> You commanded me to abstain from sleeping with a girlfriend and, in regard to marriage itself, you advised me to adopt a better way of life than you have allowed. And because you granted me strength, this was done even before I became a dispenser of your sacrament. But in my memory of which I have spoken at length, there are still live images of acts which were fixed there by my sexual habit. These images attack me. While I am awake they have no force, but in sleep they not only arouse pleasure but even elicit consent, and are very like the actual act. The illusory image within the soul has such force upon my flesh that false dreams have an effect on me when asleep, which the reality could not have when I am awake. During this time of sleep surely it is not my true self, Lord my God?[3]

In that question—"surely it is not my true self, Lord my God?"—we can detect some insecurity, some lack of certitude, and perhaps a bit of discouragement that so long after his conversion Augustine should find himself haunted by his earlier life, of which he so completely repented.

A third kind of vulnerability regarding our spiritual progress has to do with sin. To move forward on a spiritual journey, employing ascetic practices and embracing an intense life of prayer and compassionate acts, provides no guarantee that we will not sin, not fall away from the God we have claimed to love. While we live on this side of death, our love of God is not sealed. We can sin. And when we do sin, one of the consequences, especially for a dedicated and sensitive soul, is deep discouragement over the apparent lack of progress in the spiritual life.

The evil one can strike a discouraging note in our lives by telling us: "You are no different than you were before. You have not changed. You have made either little or no progress in the life journey you embraced." And we are indeed vulnerable to these discouraging messages because our spiritual progress is not easily or empirically measurable, because our memories and imagination can hold us captive to our unrepentant past, and because as long as we are alive we are capable of sin. That is the discouragement, but it is not yet the full temptation of acedia. The tempter must draw a conclusion from the discouragement and offer a plan of action. That is the voice of the devil saying: "Since you are no different and no further ahead in the spiritual journey, you might as well go back to your former way of life." For the desert fathers and mothers, "going back" meant going back to the city and all the pursuits that formed urban life then as now: making money, cultivating relationships, and enjoying entertainment. Out of discouragement, the devil is developing a scenario of returning to the familiar landscape—known and available. In the process of returning to an old and familiar way of life at the devil's prompting, however, people have also let go of their adventurous enterprise into God with all its risks and unknowns and promised satisfactions. What begins with discouragement ends in the abandonment of a graced journey into the self and God. The stakes are high. This serves as a reminder of why the demon of acedia is seen as so oppressive and dangerous.

The Second Form of Acedia: From Discouragement to Diversion

The demon might take another approach, speaking again to the Christian who has come out to the desert to follow Christ more closely and to unite himself or herself entirely to God. The evil one says:

> Look. You have come out here to this desert. And you have actually accomplished some good things. But is it enough? Could you not do so much more, if you changed your direction? Of course, you will have to leave behind some of your commitments to prayer, fasting, and other practices. But think how you could spread your spiritual wings—beyond the puny efforts that you have made. Go visit other hermits. Spend time with them. Start a new program for desert hermits. Shift gears.

In these words of the noonday demon, discouragement is very subtly embedded. For the evil one does not directly issue words of discouragement. Rather he taps into the great idealism of those who have begun to pursue a special and radically dedicated spiritual path. The implication for those whom he addresses is that they have not done all that they could do. There is more that can be accomplished than what they have mapped out with their current commitments. The idealism of devoted people who truly want to love and serve the Lord with all their hearts, with all their minds, and with all their strength is also a vulnerability. They may often feel that they have not done enough or that other horizons of commitment beckon them. In fact, these feelings reflect reality. Our finite abilities and capacities mean that there will always be more to be accomplished. Commitment, again for limited creatures like us, can always be expanded and extended in new and larger directions. All this can weigh discouragingly on the dedicated person. The logical step seems to be to do something else or to move in a different, possibly more productive direction. In fact, shifting gears because of this kind of discouragement would be a mistake, because it follows promptings of the evil one who is interested in disrupting our spiritual journey.

Saint Ignatius of Loyola has something to say about making changes in the course of discouragement. He speaks of "desolation" and means by it any turbulence, turmoil, darkness, or discouragement that the soul might feel as a person engages a deliberate and intentional journey to God, for example, through the prayer experiences of his *Spiritual Exercises*. Think, then, of the discouragement of not having done enough, a discouragement that would push us to take a different direction or action. Here is what Saint Ignatius writes:

> In time of desolation we should never make any change, but remain firm and constant in the resolution and decision which guided us the day before the desolation, or in the decision to which we adhered in the preceding consolation. For just as in consolation the good spirit guides and counsels us, so in desolation the evil spirit guides and counsels. Following his counsels we can never find the way to a right decision.[4]

An old Latin adage was dear to Saint Ignatius, and it seems to animate his advice here in the *Spiritual Exercises*. It is *age quod agis*, literally, "do what you are doing." In other words, stay the course, hold fast, and be constant. The focus in the face of the temptation to change or to do things differently—brought about by a sense of discouragement—is to remain with the task at hand, with the commitments one has already made, and with the direction that the Lord has already blessed.

The way that the discouraging temptation of acedia approaches us in this second form demonstrates a remarkable subtlety that employs our own idealism against us. It takes that idealism and makes it an engine to move us off course, away from the commitments and patterns that we have embraced on the spiritual journey—all under the guise of doing more and doing better. It is not just the desert fathers and mothers who were susceptible to this temptation. The history of spirituality gives ample evidence that every age must deal with this temptation. For example, Saint Francis de Sales in his *Introduction to the Devout Life* addresses the very same concern as he writes to his fictional reader Philothea ("lover of God"):

> The practice of devotion must be adapted to the strength, to the occupation and to the duties of each one in particular. . . . Tell me, please, my Philothea, whether it is proper for a bishop to want to lead a solitary life like a Carthusian; or for married people to be no more concerned than a Capuchin about increasing their income; or for a working man to spend his whole day in church like a religious; or on the other hand for a religious to be constantly exposed like a bishop to all the events and circumstances that bear on the needs of our neighbor. Is not this sort of devotion ridiculous, unorganized and intolerable? Yet this absurd error occurs very frequently, but in no way does true devotion, my Philothea, destroy anything at all. On the contrary, it perfects and fulfills all things.[5]

The second form of the temptation of acedia is to move from an idealism that breeds discouragement to do something different or other than one's present commitment. Again, the oppressive and threatening noonday demon of acedia presents a very significant danger that threatens to divert us on the journey to God and possibly to derail the journey entirely by getting us to "do something different."

The Third Form of Acedia: From Discouragement to Paralysis

The third way that the noonday devil might approach the ascetics of the desert began as the first way—with discouraging words. Then the devil moved in a somewhat different way with the discouragement. Again, we listen in to the voice of the evil one:

Look at you. It is some time now that you have come out to the desert to find God. You have read the Bible. You have denied yourself food and sleep. You have tried to pray constantly. But be honest with yourself. You still have the same bad thoughts that haunt you. You still have the nasty inclinations that you so wanted to be rid of. You still have the same small heart. And let me tell you something. It is not that you have not tried. You surely have tried your best. I will tell you the problem. You just cannot do it. You do not have the ability to change. Whatever you do, it will never work. So, just give up. Yes, just give up. Forget about this "spiritual quest" and all the other fine and holy things you have thought up. It is not going to happen—ever.

Notice the line of thinking that the devil introduces. He begins as he began in the first way of acedia by identifying the lack of progress in the ascetic's life. Along the way, he employs a number of spiritual fallacies and deceptions, as one might expect. He implies that since a soul is not perfectly ordered in its thoughts, inclinations, and compassion, there is no progress, and that is not true. In his assessment of the soul in question, he fallaciously implies that the only real progress on the spiritual journey is to have arrived at one's heavenly destination, complete and perfect. In effect, he denies the journey or pilgrimage character of our lives in God. He falsely lays out the alternatives: full progress or no progress.

Then the evil one inserts his most insidious deception into his description of the soul's progress. Quite clearly, he says: "You just cannot do it. You do not have the ability to change. Whatever you do, it will never work." He implies that the work of change or transformation is the work of the believer who embarks on the spiritual journey and that the believer is the one ultimately responsible for whatever happens. Cleverly concealed in these words is an outright denial of the grace of God, which alone has the power to transform us and make us new creatures. The counterpoint to this is Saint Paul's insistence that we are saved by grace. So we read in the Letter to the Ephesians:

> God, who is rich in mercy, out of the great love with which
> he loved us even when we were dead through our trespass-
> es, made us alive together with Christ—by grace you have
> been saved—and raised us up with him. . . . For by grace
> you have been saved through faith, and this is not your own
> doing; it is the gift of God—not the result of works, so that
> no one may boast. (2:4–6, 8–9)

The overall message of the evil one is that there is no future and
no potential for the journey. That is, indeed, a very discouraging message. He takes it to a next step, its practical implication. What do we
do when we recognize that the future holds no promise and that we do
not have the capacity to make a difference? The devil's practical conclusion is clear and logical: "Just give up. Forget about this 'spiritual
quest' and all the other fine and holy things you have thought up." The
devil, in other words, leads us to embrace paralysis, immobility, and a
full-fledged succumbing to discouragement.

This form of acedia is at least as dangerous as the other two because, if one succumbs to it, the entire spiritual journey is derailed by
bringing it to a complete halt. In fact, this form of acedia seems to me
to be the most dangerous of the three. The first form, regression, and
the second form, diversion, do not cut off all possibilities. The third
form of immobilization or paralysis effectively and entirely blocks the
future.

This discouraging form of acedia that would halt us entirely on the
spiritual journey affects souls who have made, with God's help, notable
strides in their lives. For example, Saint Teresa of Avila opened a new
chapter in her spiritual journey when she sought to found a new and
reformed house for her community. As she began to move in that direction, the devil tried to discourage her in such a way that the entire
project would be stopped. She describes what happened:

> The devil raised doubts in me also about how I wanted to
> shut myself up in so austere a house, and with my many ill-
> nesses. How would I able to endure so much penance and

leave a monastery that was large and pleasant and where I had always been so happy? And how could I leave so many friends, for perhaps those in the new house would not be to my liking? I had obligated myself to a great deal; perhaps I would despair. The devil by chance may have intended to take away my peace and quiet so that on account of such disturbance I wouldn't be able to pay and thus would lose my soul. Thoughts of this sort, all mixed together, he put before my mind; I was powerless to think of anything else. This state was accompanied by an affliction and obscurity and darkness of soul that I wouldn't know how to exaggerate. Finding myself in such a condition, I made a visit to the Blessed Sacrament; although I couldn't pray. It seems to me the anguish I experienced was like that of someone in the death agony. . . . Oh, God help me, what a miserable life this is![6]

Notice the elements of temptation that Saint Teresa experienced. They are the elements of discouragement that the devil incites by pointing out to her all her inadequacies and inabilities. She is left spiritually paralyzed, not even able to pray before the Blessed Sacrament. She does, however, lift up a simple cry for help: "Oh God, help me." And God does hear her prayer in the midst of the temptation. God gives her the gift of knowing where this discouragement is coming from—the devil. God also directs her response to the temptation. The temptation is to give up, and the response is to recommit to the path that was chosen. She writes:

Never did [God] fail to succor me in my tribulations. And He did so in my present one, for He gave me a little light to enable me to see it was the devil and to understand the truth that it was all due to the devil's desire to frighten me with lies. As a result I began to recall my strong resolutions to serve the Lord and my desires to suffer for Him. . . . [I reflected] that I had nothing to fear, for since I desired the trials, these troubles were good; that the greater the opposition the greater the gain. And why did I lack courage to serve one whom I owed so much?[7]

To hear the story of Saint Teresa's encounter with the temptation of acedia that sought to discourage her and paralyze her on the journey is both comforting and frightening. We find some comfort in knowing that even a great soul such as Saint Teresa underwent experiences that can easily belong to us as well. We also find it frightening to think that no one seems spared this kind of difficult testing. Further reflection may also lead us to conclude how appropriate it is that we daily pray: "Lead us not into temptation but deliver us from evil."

Acedia as an Individual and Communal Experience

The temptation of acedia stirs a common sense of discouragement but takes on a distinctive threefold form: regression (go back), diversion (do something else), and paralysis (collapse in your own sadness). As we have considered acedia and the devil's work of discouragement connected with it, we have spoken of individuals who have been so affected and afflicted. More specifically, we have understood how individuals who have embarked on an intentional spiritual journey are susceptible to the temptation of acedia—discouragement some time after they have been on the journey. There is also a way that acedia in its triple form affects not only individuals but groups of people and communities who are on a journey together.

This is particularly evident in the story of Israel in Exodus from Egypt and on the way to the promised land. God frees the people of Israel from the slavery of Egypt. They march triumphantly across the Red Sea. It is the beginning of the journey of freedom, and an exhilarating journey it is. After they cross the Red Sea, the Book of Exodus recounts the song that Moses and the Israelites sang:

> I will sing to the Lord, for he has triumphed gloriously; horse and rider he has thrown into the sea. The Lord is my strength and my might, and he has become my salvation; this is my God, and I will praise him, my father's God, and I will exalt him. The Lord is a warrior; the Lord is his name. (15:1–3; see 15:4–18)

Then the journey through the desert begins. After they have been on the journey for a while, they experience the threefold temptation of acedia-discouragement, as we saw it played out in the journeys of individuals. First, they·complain to Moses: "Why did you bring us here into this desert? When we were in Egypt, we were slaves, of course, but we knew the food, had our shelter, and followed our routines. Here in this trackless wasteland, there is none of that. Why don't we go back?" So, the first form of the temptation for the people in Exodus is to go back to their enslavement.

The second form of the temptation of acedia occurs as well. Moses is on the mountain, and the people wonder about him and about their destiny. They plan to do things in another way. They speak with Aaron: "We don't know where Moses is or if he will return. And if he returns will he truly lead us forward. Why don't we try something else? Let's build a golden calf." Wearied with the journey and unsure of Moses' leadership, they fall into the second form of the temptation of acedia—to do something else, to move off the plan and pattern of their original commitment and God's plan for them.

Finally, as the Israelites make their way through the desert, they are overcome with a sense of futility and a communal depression. Everything turns bleak. Nothing seems possible. The discouragement is such that it paralyzes them. They feel that they might as well sit down in the desert and die, because they feel no hope and have no sense of a future. This is the third form of the temptation of acedia-discouragement—to fall into a sadness that lays them low, halts them on the journey, and immobilizes them.

The collective experience of acedia-discouragement can obviously continue today, especially in communities of faith. Elements of this collective form of acedia are evident in the Church in the context of the renewal initiated by the Second Vatican Council. The journey of renewal has not been smooth. Some voices call for a return to or restoration of things as they were, the first form of acedia that leads to regression. Others see the insufficiency of the renewal and call for a program of radical reconfiguration of the Church, the second form of acedia that leads to diversion or doing another thing. Finally, some are so taken by the difficulties and the confusion that they feel themselves paralyzed on the journey, the third form of acedia that involves collapse into sadness. Although these examples are drawn from the life of the larger Church, the same temptation can afflict a smaller church community on its spiritual journey as well.

The response to the discouragement that acedia introduces to the journey—whether individual or collective—falls under a more general response to discouragement that we will consider at the end of this chapter. The desert monastics suggested an intensification of effort in the various ascetic practices and certainly an intensification of prayer. No one of them, however, had a surefire formula for banishing the noonday demon. After we consider other forms of discouragement that the devil might introduce into our lives or discouragement that may well arise from within us, I will suggest a response based on a theology and experience of the cross of Jesus. As we shall see, it is a response and not a resolution. Until we have taken our last breath, we must continue to pray from the heart, "Lead us not into temptation but deliver us from evil."

Discouragement Due to Tiredness

Acedia, as we have considered it and as it emerges in the spiritual tradition of the desert, especially affects those on an intentional spiritual journey with a dangerous temptation to discouragement. In fact, the bane of discouragement touches us in many particular contexts. And in every way, the devil can use it to push us away from God. In the following sections, we will consider some particular forms that discouragement takes, beginning with discouragement due to tiredness.

Weariness can and does take hold of us. We are, after all, finite creatures and we get tired. The dimension of temptation enters into tiredness when the evil one takes that tiredness and uses it as a signal to us that we should move away from doing what we are called to do.

He pulls us, in other words, into a disheartened and discouraged state and then toward the abandonment of our commitments or what is entrusted to us.

See how this process unfolds in the life of Moses:

> Moses heard the people weeping throughout their families, all at the entrances of their tents. Then the Lord became very angry, and Moses was displeased. So Moses said to the Lord, "Why have you treated your servant badly? Why have I not found favor in your sight, that you lay the burden of all this people on me? Did I conceive all this people? Did I give birth to them, that you should say to me, 'Carry them in your bosom, as a nurse carries a sucking child,' to the land that you promised on oath to their ancestors? Where am I to get meat to give to all this people? For they come weeping to me and say, 'Give us meat to eat!' I am not able to carry all this people alone, for they are too heavy for me. If this is the way you are going to treat me, put me to death at once—if I have found favor in your sight—and not let me see my misery." (Numbers 11:10–15)

The tiredness of Moses triggers discouragement that, in turn, leads him to want to escape it all by death. Although Moses' situation and responsibility are unique, we know all too well elements of this same pattern in our lives and the lives of those we know. Severely ill people undergoing treatment for their illness often suffer a discouraging weariness that prompts them to want to abandon their course of treatment and just give up, even if there is a prospect for improvement.

Another form of this discouraging tiredness affects those who have committed themselves to the compassionate care of others. Their commitment is very good and, one could even say, noble. After a while, however, the responsibilities of care and the emotional drain take their toll. They begin to experience what is often called compassion fatigue. This can happen to medical personnel or those engaged in working with the poor or socially marginalized. It can also happen to those who engage in compassion "part time," that is, people of means who try their best to share generously of their resources with others. The unceasing needs and demands have a wearying effect and incline people to stop what they began.

Again, it is important to note that weariness or tiredness is a natural consequence of work or personal investment. There is no evil or sin in that. The devil's interest in our tiredness is to move us to decide to give up entirely the good involvement that we have taken on.

Besides the more general response to discouragement, which we will consider later, we can address the particular discouragement that arises from tiredness in several ways. A sharing of the burden is a first possibility. This is what happened for Moses with the gathering of the seventy elders to assist him (see Numbers 11:16–30). Another response to tiredness is rest. Jesus himself summons his disciples to rest or to a form of Sabbath time:

> The apostles gathered around Jesus, and told him all that they had done and taught. He said to them, "Come away to a deserted place all by yourselves and rest a while." For many were coming and going, and they had no leisure even to eat. And they went away in the boat to a deserted place by themselves. (Mark 6:30–32)

A third response to the discouraging tiredness that might lead us to give up is a remembrance of the good things the Lord has done that leads to thanksgiving and that, in turn, leads to recommitment. This is evident in Psalm 116:

> The Lord protects the simple; when I was brought low, he saved me. Return, O my soul, to your rest, for the Lord has dealt bountifully with you. . . . I have kept my faith, even when I said, "I am greatly afflicted." . . . What shall I return to the Lord for all his bounty to me? I will lift up the cup of salvation and call on the name of the Lord. (vv. 6–7, 10, 12–13)

In a tired or wearied state, our defenses and our alertness are down. This provides the evil one with a special opportunity to foster discouragement and lead people away from important commitments. Some initial responses include burden-sharing, rest, and recommitment rooted in gratitude.

Discouragement Due to a Sense of Being Overwhelmed

There is a mysterious passage in Paul's Second Letter to the Corinthians that commentators have never been able to fully explain. Paul writes about an affliction of some kind that seems to overwhelm him. Whatever it is, it discourages him. He sees the hand of Satan in it. And again, whatever it is, it propels him into the hands of God. We read:

> To keep me from being too elated, a thorn was given me in the flesh, a messenger of Satan to torment me, to keep me from being too elated. Three times I appealed to the Lord about this, that it would leave me, but he said to me, "My grace is sufficient for you, for power is made perfect in weakness." (12:7–9)

The sense of being overwhelmed touches the lives of many people. A feeling of powerlessness, for example, marks the lives of those who struggle with various forms of addiction, as we saw earlier. That same feeling of powerlessness can also arise from sets of life circumstances that seem to conspire to confuse us and hold us down. Those circumstances may include our interpersonal, occupational, economic, and social worlds. The people closest to us seem out of reach. Our jobs make demands on us of a quality and quantity that we can never hope to meet them. Our finances put us on the brink of insecurity. We feel isolated and tremendously alone in life. These are the circumstances that make us feel overwhelmed.

It is an easy move from being overwhelmed and feeling powerless to a deep sense of discouragement that disengages us from other people, our very selves, and—of course—God. The evil one fosters the move toward disengagement by using the discouragement arising from a sense of powerlessness and the feeling of being overwhelmed.

Disengagement marks a triumph of sin, because sin always entails a separation from others, self, and God.

Facing one's own powerlessness requires courage, but it is exactly courage that is lacking because of powerlessness. For Paul, this vicious circle is broken only when he hears God's voice speak to him in the midst of his weakness: "My grace is sufficient for you, for power is made perfect in weakness" (2 Corinthians 12:9). For Paul or for any of us who sense our own powerlessness, courage comes not from within us but in an act of reliance on the one who is all-powerful.

Discouragement Due to Intimidation

Fear shapes human behavior and does so powerfully. Jesus regularly admonishes his disciples: "Do not be afraid." His words hold a special weight for his followers who, according to their master, will inevitably encounter hostility, persecution, and all forms of intimidating circumstances. The tenth chapter of Matthew's Gospel represents a *vademecum,* or handbook for missionaries in the early Church. Jesus prepares his disciples for intimidation:

> See, I am sending you out like sheep into the midst of wolves; so be wise as serpents and innocent as doves. Beware of them, for they will hand you over to councils and flog you in their synagogues; and you will be dragged before governors and kings because of me, as a testimony to them and the Gentiles. When they hand you over, do not worry about how you are to speak or what you are to say; for what you are to say will be given to you at that time; for it is not you who will speak, but the Spirit of your Father speaking through you. Brother will betray brother to death, and a father his child, and children will rise against parent and have them put to death; and you will be hated by all because of my name. But the one who endures to the end will be saved. When they persecute you in one town, flee to the next; for truly I tell you, you will not have gone through all the towns of Israel before the Son of Man comes. (10:16–23)

The persecution and the intimidation that Jesus indicates could easily lead to great discouragement. That discouragement, in turn, can cause us to buckle under and move away from the clear and uncompromising proclamation of faith. This would represent our failure and the devil's triumph. So, it is important to understand the state of discouragement that can be the prelude to abandoning the holy tasks entrusted to us.

In the context of intimidation and persecution, believers stand at the intersection of the devil's discouraging influence. The evil one is at work both in those who intimidate and persecute God's holy ones and in the souls of those who experience being intimidated and persecuted. The devil encourages persecutors and discourages those who are persecuted. The devil's hope is to halt the proclamation of God's word and so to thwart the coming of God's reign in this broken and needy world. In his plan of attack, he can single out, of course, those who are the designated missionaries bringing the good news of Jesus Christ to those who have not yet heard his name or who have only begun to hear it. The evil one can stir up regimes (and has) that may be threatened by the sovereignty of God signified by the proclamation of the coming of the reign of God. For all these macro-movements, there are also countless other micro-instances of individuals who want to give witness to Jesus Christ in a more personal way but find themselves intimidated by forces well beyond their control. This could be, for example, an individual in a commercial enterprise who stands up for justice and fairness.

The Gospel suggests a remedy for the discouragement that is brought on by fear. It proposes that one's fears be properly aligned: fear God, not human beings (see Matthew 10:28). The Gospel also suggests confidence in the presence of the Holy Spirit, who will lead, guide, and direct those who experience persecution and discouragement (see Matthew 10:19–20). Finally, the Gospel promotes identification with Jesus Christ: "A disciple is not above the teacher, nor a slave above the master; it is enough for the disciple to be like the teacher, and the slave like the master" (Matthew 10:24–25).

Discouragement Due to Personal Disappointment

Personal disappointment means that we disappoint ourselves. We have certain goals and aspirations for ourselves, and we fail to meet them. The result is disappointment. We have a certain self-ideal, a sense of how we should or ought to be, and yet we live at variance with that sense of self. Again, the result is disappointment. When these disappointments are replayed frequently over time, they breed a sense of discouragement. This can be a devastating experience. We lose heart about ourselves. The discouragement is then compounded, because we cannot walk away from ourselves. If we encounter discouraging situations or circumstances, although it may not be good to step back, often we can do so. If we regularly encounter within ourselves sources of ongoing disappointment and, therefore, discouragement, we cannot walk away. Even more distressing, we may not even be able to continue walking at all. In the hands of the evil one, personal disappointment and its attendant sense of discouragement are artfully manipulated, so we have a feeling of being boxed in, with nowhere to go, and so far from God.

Personal disappointment joined to deep discouragement seems to have overtaken Judas Iscariot after he saw what he had done to Jesus. He tried to make some form of restitution but found himself stymied. He had nowhere to go. He exited in the only way he sensed he could:

> When Judas, his betrayer, saw that Jesus was condemned, he repented and brought back the thirty pieces of silver to the chief priests and the elders. He said, "I have sinned by betraying innocent blood." But they said, "What is that to us? See to it yourself." Throwing down the pieces of silver in the temple, he departed; and he went and hanged himself. (Matthew 27:3–5)

The logic of the devil who "had already put it into the heart of Judas son of Simon Iscariot to betray him" (John 13:2) leads ruinously from disappointment to discouragement to death. The logic of God leads from disappointment to discouragement to hope, not in oneself but God, and finally, to repentance and new life.

As a confessor and spiritual director, I have walked with many people who struggle with personal disappointment, the deep, abiding, and sometimes constant sense of having disappointed themselves by not living up to what makes up their aspirations. Frequently, this disappointment accompanies a pattern of habitual sin. It may be a sexual matter, or it may be a persistent sense of anger or irritation directed to the same person. The penitent does not want to keep repeating the pattern of sinful behavior but seems powerless to stop. Each time the sinful behavior occurs, the sense of self-recrimination widens and deepens. It can seem to come to a breaking point of despair and total abandonment of basic commitments.

In this context, penitents are very much absorbed in the sinful behavior that they are unable to control. More than absorbed, they can become fixated and even obsessed by it. As a confessor or spiritual director, I receive their confessions or admissions of failure. In other words, I take the confession of their sins seriously. I do not consider it as a matter of regrettable but habitual behavior for which there is less culpability. At the same time, I take great pains to highlight what I see as the danger greater than their particular sin. It is the deep discouragement that could entirely subvert their relationship with God, perhaps by foreclosing—in their minds—even the possibility of their repentance. These are painful and, at times, confusing conversations, because there is so much at stake. It is a matter of penetrating layers of the self until, ultimately, we come to the center. There and then, we learn to say yes to God in trust. This grace-filled trust transcends our own sense of disappointment in ourselves and our utter lack of confidence in our own capacity to stay with the right thing and to do it.

These moments of profound self-disappointment make us vulnerable to the machinations of the devil, who can easily lead us away from God on the path of discouragement. He does so by introducing us to the spiritual fallacy that we are the ones responsible for our own virtue and holiness. He convinces us to put confidence in ourselves and to ignore the true object of our trust in God. The antidote to this toxic and ruinous fallacy is to learn a new and authentic way of confidence. A most remarkable prayer of Saint Claude de la Colombière—*An Act of Confidence in God*—serves as a school of true trust:

> My God, I am so convinced that you keep watch over those who hope in you, and that we can want for nothing when we look for all from you, that I am resolved in the future to live free from every care, and to turn all my anxieties over to you. "In peace, in the selfsame, I will sleep and I will rest; for thou, O Lord, singularly hast settled me in hope" (Psalm 4:9–10). Men may deprive me of possessions and of honor; sickness may strip me of strength and the means of serving you; I may even lose your grace by sin; but I shall never lose my hope. I shall keep it till the last moment of my life; and at that moment all the demons in hell shall strive to tear it from me in vain. "In peace, in the selfsame, I will sleep and I will rest." Others may look for happiness from their wealth or their talents; others may rest on the innocence of their life, or the severity of their penance, or the amount of their alms, or the fervor of their prayers. "Thou, O Lord, singularly hast settled me in hope." As for me, Lord, all my confidence is my confidence itself. This confidence has never deceived anyone. No one, no one has hoped in the Lord and has been confounded. I am sure, therefore, that I shall be eternally happy, since I firmly hope to be, and because it is from you, O God, that I hope for it. "In thee, O Lord, have I hoped; let me never be confounded" (Psalm 30:1). I know, alas! I know only too well, that I am weak and unstable. I know what temptation can do against the strongest virtue. I have seen the stars of heaven fall, and the pillars of the firmament; but that cannot frighten me. So long as I continue to hope, I shall be sheltered from all misfortune; and I am sure of hoping always, since I hope

also for this unwavering hopefulness. Finally, I am sure that I cannot hope too much in you, and that I cannot receive less than I have hoped for from you. So I hope that you will hold me safe on the steepest slopes, that you will sustain me against the most furious assaults, and that you will make my weakness triumph over my most fearful enemies. I hope that you will love me always, and that I too shall love you without ceasing. To carry my hope once for all as far as it can go, I hope from you to possess you, O my Creator, in time and in eternity. Amen.

This remarkable prayer draws us beyond the struggle with self and the struggle with the discouraging demonic voices that promise only doom. The prayer recenters our source of confidence in God and so enables us to be free of ourselves in a great act of surrender.

Discouragement Due to the Ineffectiveness of Effecting Change

Discouragement, as we noted earlier, often affects people who are particularly idealistic and who want to do good things with their lives. Precisely because they know what could be and have a sense of a potential future, the failure to realize these aspirations gives rise to their discouragement. Those, for example, who dedicate themselves to care for the poor or the marginalized are motivated by a vision of possibility. When repeated efforts show no significant change in the plight of the people who are served, then possibility seems to become impossibility, and discouragement arises. With discouragement, of course, comes the evil one's suggestion to abandon the project, whatever it might be.

Religiously minded people who commit themselves to some form of ministry to their brothers and sisters are especially prone to this kind of discouragement. The results of ministerial investment rarely match the expectations. The timelines of the one serving and the actual moment of impact on those served may vary considerably. In other words, ministry may plant a seed that takes more time and patience than we would have anticipated to bear fruit. The prospect of walking away from one's ministerial commitment seems inviting, since results are not forthcoming. Adjustments and adaptations of one kind or another belong to a normal part of life and ministry. Walking away from a commitment because of deep discouragement at the lack of results does not.

A striking example of meeting and responding to this temptation to walk away because of discouraging results can be found in the life of Charles de Foucauld. This one-time French foreign legionnaire underwent a profound conversion and transformation from a worldly life of soldiering to the dedicated, ascetic life of a monk-hermit. He died in 1916 at the hands of rebel members of a North African tribe that he had gone to serve. His strategy had been a simple one—to bring Christ to the desert.

Charles de Foucauld described his vision and what he would do. In fact, he implemented this vision not with a community but by himself in holy solitude in the Sahara. He wrote:

> We wish to found . . . a small, humble hermitage, where a few poor monks live on a little fruit and barley harvested with their own hands. They would live in a small, narrow enclosure in the penitence and adoration of the Holy Sacrament, never leaving and never preaching, but giving hospitality to anyone who comes, good or bad, friend or enemy, Moslem or Christian. This is Evangelism not by talk, but by the presence of the Very Holy Sacrament and the offer of the Divine Sacrifice, prayer, penitence, the practice of Evangelical virtues, charity—a charity that is fraternal and universal, sharing the last crust of bread with every pauper, every guest, every stranger who comes, and receiving every human being as a beloved brother.[8]

The vision of Charles de Foucauld was fundamentally to replicate Nazareth, the place of the hidden life of Jesus that was full of his presence. There were very few results that Charles de Foucauld could point to. He stayed with his commitment, and he stayed in his beloved Nazareth in the Sahara and with those who dwelled there. The following reflection expresses a question that suggests he faced disappointment and discouragement. He met that challenge by more deeply committing himself to do what he had pledged to do.

> Does my presence do any good here? Contact with the natives helps to lessen the feeling of strangeness, tames them, and slowly makes taboos and prejudices disappear. It is very slow, a very little thing. It is painful to see the reign of evil all around, the lack of good, the enemies of the Lord who are so enterprising, the friends who are so faltering, and to see oneself so miserable after so many blessings. However, one should not be sad but should look above it all, to our Beloved Lord. For it is he whom we love and not ourselves, and it is his good that concerns us. Hope is a duty—charity hopes for all—hope is but faith in the goodness of God. He is good and all-powerful. Unquestionably, he leaves us free, and often we use our freedom lamentably, but while leaving us free, he still remains the master and can at his will send a grace so powerful that it overwhelms everything, transforms everything. He has already done enough for us to make us believe in his love.[9]

As he carries on his work and presence in the desert, Charles de Foucauld is clearly conscious of the link between discouragement and the devil and the need to address that insidious temptation with simple directness: "We must work continuously, without becoming discouraged, against ourselves, the world, and the Devil until the end of time. Act, pray, and suffer—these are our methods."[10]

Besides the manifestations of discouragement in the temptation of acedia, we have considered the link between discouragement and several related experiences: tiredness, a sense of being overwhelmed, intimidation, personal disappointment, and the disappointment of not being able to effect the change we would like. Taken together, these experiences reflect a fundamental poverty of our human spirit. By dint of our own forces, we are just not up to implementing the great aspirations of our hearts. We are basically poor. There is no news in that. Our poverty is another expression of our finite being. The evil one, however, can capitalize on our poverty. In a right ordering of things, our poverty ought to drive us closer to the one on whom we entirely depend—God, who is the fullness of being. The devil's suggestion pushes us in the opposite direction. He reinforces our sense of the gap between God and us, between the infinite and the finite. He tells us that the gap is unbridgeable and that we might as well fall back into our own finitude, perhaps even into our own nothingness. That is the devil's message of discouragement, meant to move us away from God, who calls us forward to himself. And that message can be quite effective.

To understand a holy response to this unholy temptation to move away from God because of discouragement, we turn to the word of God that anchors our confidence in Jesus Christ. First, we will consider several specific responses in the New Testament, and then conclude with Jesus on the cross.

Response to Discouragement: Paul in Mission and Ministry

Paul's most sustained and personal reflection on his mission and ministry appears in his Second Letter to the Corinthians. He shares with the Corinthian community both his struggles and his sustaining hope. The following selection characterizes what he is dealing with in the course of ministry and how he deals with it:

> But we have this treasure in clay jars, so that it may be made clear that this extraordinary power belongs to God and does not come from us. We are afflicted in every way, but not crushed; perplexed, but not driven to despair; persecuted, but not forsaken; struck down, but not destroyed; always carrying in the body of the death of Jesus, so that the life of Jesus may also be made visible in our bodies. For while we live, we are always being given up to death for Jesus' sake, so that the life of Jesus may be made visible in our mortal flesh. So death is at work in us, but life in you. . . . So we do not lose heart. Even though our outer

> nature is wasting away, our inner nature is being renewed day by day. For this slight momentary affliction is preparing us for an eternal weight of glory beyond all measure. (4:7–12, 16–17)

Not surprisingly, Paul's words contain a density of thought and experience that needs some explication. These few verses do look at the phenomenon of discouragement in a mission-ministry context, but they avoid any kind of glib response. Paul does not immediately summon an encouraging answer to discouraging situations. Rather, he carefully identifies the sustaining power that enables him to carry on what God has entrusted to him. He does so by noting the fundamental assumption of his ministry, the real experience of struggle, the Christocentric purpose of that struggle, and the horizon beyond the struggle.

Paul assumes that his weakness, manifest in the struggle with the difficult circumstances of mission and ministry and its attendant discouragement, belongs to the overall drama of our salvation. In other words, as Paul often proclaims, our weakness manifests God's power and the primacy of grace. We are not the responsible agents for our salvation. It is all God's doing. And so we must assume that our fragile condition and our struggles are part of that pattern.

Then, in a few words that compress a great deal of apostolic experience, Paul describes the real struggle of his mission and ministry. At the same time, he clearly notes that he has always found himself sustained and carried forward, not cast down and not halted in doing what he was to do, as one might expect from the difficulties he encountered. So, he is describing real struggle but also a struggle in which he is sustained. "We are afflicted in every way, but not crushed; perplexed, but not driven to despair; persecuted but not destroyed" (2 Corinthians 4:8–9).

The key, then, to Paul's capacity to stay sustained and encouraged in the course of his struggles is the holy purpose of those struggles: the manifestation of the death and life of the Lord Jesus. Through this experience of the death and resurrection of the Lord, Paul becomes the effective instrument—in this death-like struggle—to communicate to the Corinthians the very life of Jesus. He is clearly anchored in this holy purpose, even as he says to the Corinthians: "Yes, everything is for your sake, so that grace, as it extends to more and more people, may increase thanksgiving, to the glory of God" (2 Corinthians 4:15).

A last source of sustenance and encouragement rests in the future that Paul glimpses. This is the horizon beyond the suffering of the pres-ent moment. Just as discouragement tends to collapse everything into the present moment, making us feel that our current struggle is forever, so Paul breaks free of this spiritual implosion by envisioning the hope that lies ahead: "For this slight momentary affliction is preparing us for an eternal weight of glory beyond all measure" (2 Corinthians 4:17).

This evocation of Paul's experience in his mission and ministry is meant to help us formulate our own response to discouragement, lest the devil push us away from God. Our life circumstances, obviously, do not coincide with those of Paul. Still, there are extraordinary, useful elements that can speak to our struggles and our temptations arising from discouragement. Paul's assumption, for example, of his weakness as a vehicle to manifest God's power helps us remember what we often forget: that we ought not to be surprised by struggle or the experience of discouragement, and that God's actions and not our own remedies will ultimately prevail. Paul's description of struggles that can easily induce a sense of discouragement moves us to a realistic assessment of our situation. He does not mask things, and we ought not do so, either. His centering on the holy purpose of communicating the death and resurrection of Jesus to others sustains and encourages him, and so can the Christocentric purpose of our struggles keep us encouraged as we move forward. We may need to explore and probe the relationship between our particular struggles and the death and resurrection of the Lord Jesus, but we are convinced that there is a relationship. Through baptism, after all, we have been united with him in a death like his so that we can be united with him in a resurrection like his (see Romans 6:5). That union will shape and affect all the particular elements of our lives, including our struggles. Finally, with Paul in the midst of struggles that carry strong potential for discouragement, we break from the present moment to glimpse the horizon of glory ahead of us.

Response to Discouragement: The Letter to the Hebrews

The Letter to the Hebrews was written as a message of exhortation or encouragement (see Hebrews 13:22) directed to Christians who were weary. The writer summons these faltering spirits to reclaim their original commitment. The following passages suggest paths of finding encouragement:

> Therefore, my friends, since we have confidence to enter the sanctuary by the blood of Jesus . . . let us hold fast to the confession of our hope without wavering, for he who has promised is faithful. And let us consider how to provoke one another to love and good deeds, not neglecting to meet together, as is the habit of some, but encouraging one another, and all the more as you see the Day approaching. . . . But recall those earlier days when, after you had been enlightened, you endured a hard struggle with sufferings, sometimes being publicly exposed to abuse and persecution, and sometimes being partners with those so treated. For you had compassion for those who were in prison, and you cheerfully accepted the plundering of your possessions, knowing that you yourselves possessed something better and more lasting. Do not, therefore, abandon that confidence of yours; it brings a great reward. For you need endurance, so that when you have done the will of God, you may receive what was promised. . . . Therefore, since we are surrounded by so great a cloud of witnesses, let us also lay aside every weight and the sin that clings so closely, and let us run with perseverance the race that is set before us, looking to Jesus the pioneer and perfecter of our faith, who for the sake of the joy that was set before him endured the cross, disregarding its shame, and has taken his seat at the right hand of the throne of God. (10:19, 23–25, 32–36; 12:1–2)

These selections from the Letter to the Hebrews offer a path of encouragement that echoes Paul's words in his Second Letter to the Corinthians. For example, Hebrews exhorts its readers to keep their eyes fixed on Jesus, who shows a path through suffering to glory. The letter also tells readers to look ahead to the day of the Lord and the destiny that God holds for us.

In addition to Paul's reflections, Hebrews adds two responses to the listlessness and discouragement that can afflict the followers of Jesus. The letter invites readers to encourage one another. The community brought together by the reconciling sacrifice of Jesus Christ can itself become a powerful resource in addressing the challenge of discouragement: "Provoke one another to love and good deeds . . . encouraging one another" (10:24–25). Although not explicitly noted in the letter, the evil one's use of discouragement to impede the journey to God in fidelity and perseverance is certainly in the background. The source of encouragement, the letter affirms, can be found in the community as a whole that stays faithful and supportive. The second response suggested by Hebrews is to recall original commitments and first struggles: "Recall those earlier days when, after you had been enlightened, you endured a hard struggle with sufferings" (10:32). Contained in this appeal to remember is also an invitation to renew a commitment. The recovery of our origins in the Christian life, the letter seems to suggest, can help us refocus in our current state of struggle and possible discouragement.

Response to Discouragement: The Book of Revelation

The Book of Revelation is notoriously difficult to understand because of its complex, apocalyptic language and intricate symbolism. In contrast to the complexity of its style, the purpose of the Book of Revelation is quite simple. It was meant to be an encouragement to Christians who found themselves in a state of crisis because of the persecutions of the early Church. In fact, its message remains valid for Christians of all generations, because whatever the historical epoch,

Christians will face crisis in one way or another. The Book of Revelation offers a fundamental encouragement by proclaiming the victory of Jesus Christ. A clear example of the message emerges in the account of Michael's defeat of the dragon:

> And war broke out in heaven; Michael and his angels fought against the dragon. The dragon and his angels fought back, but they were defeated, and there was no longer any place for them in heaven. The great dragon was thrown down, that ancient serpent, who is called the Devil and Satan, the deceiver of the whole world—he was thrown down to the earth, and his angels were thrown down with him. Then I heard a loud voice in heaven, proclaiming, "Now have come the salvation and the power and the kingdom of our God and the authority of his Messiah, for the accuser of our comrades has been thrown down, who accuses them day and night before our God. But they have conquered him by the blood of the Lamb and by the word of their testimony, for they did not cling to life even in the face of death. Rejoice then, you heavens and those who dwell in them! But woe to the earth and the sea, for the devil has come down to you with great wrath, because he knows that his time is short!" (12:7–12)

This passage, addressed to those who are suffering persecution and hardship for their faith, identifies the culprit behind these painful and discouraging difficulties. It is "that ancient serpent, who is called the Devil and Satan, the deceiver of the whole world." The devil is also identified as "the accuser of our comrades [or alternately, "our brothers"] . . . who accuses them day and night before our God." Besides engineering the persecution of God's faithful ones, the evil one accuses them in the heavenly court. He is bent on their ruin. These verses clearly describe the link of troubles, discouragement, and attempts to bring Christians to ruin—all connected to the devil's agency. In describing this, however, Revelation also proclaims the reason for encouragement. That encouragement stems from the definitive victory of God signaled by the blood of Jesus, the blood of the Lamb. The

victory is given and assured, and it is something in which those persecuted even to the point of death share, the ones who "did not cling to
life even in the face of death."

The definitive victory in Jesus Christ, however, does not dispense
us from continuing to struggle until the end of time. While we are in
time and until we are in eternity, the devil can still wreak his mischief
on the earth and the sea. He does come "with great wrath, because he
knows that his time is short." At the end of time, the faithful followers
of Jesus Christ will share fully in his definitive victory. In other words,
the devil wants us away from God and uses struggles to discourage us
and so move us in the direction that he wants. In fact, the blood of
Jesus Christ has already won our victory over the devil, a victory that
we can fully claim at the end of time. In the meanwhile, our source of
encouragement is in the victory that God gives us in Jesus Christ and
the promised future that will be ours if we stay faithful. This fact and
this promise enable us to stay the course.

Response to Discouragement: The Gospel of John

As John portrays Jesus at the Last Supper, Jesus speaks what is deepest
in his heart as he prepares his disciples for his departure. He invites
them to be servants of one another, to love each other, and to be one
as he is one with the Father. In his discourse, Jesus also prepares the
disciples for struggles that they will encounter and the discouragement
that will accompany those struggles. He says:

> If the world hates you, be aware that it hated me before it
> hated you. If you belonged to the world, the world would
> love you as its own. Because you do not belong to the
> world, but I have chosen you out of the world—therefore
> the world hates you. Remember the word that I said to you,
> "Servants are not greater than their master." If they per-
> secuted me, they will persecute you. . . . I have said these
> things to you so that when their hour comes you may re-
> member that I told you about them. . . . I have said this to
> you, so that in me you may have peace. In the world you

> face persecution. But take courage; I have conquered the
> world. (15:18–20; 16:4, 33)

Jesus anticipates with his disciples the future struggles that await them. His purpose is reassurance, but he knows that they face the prospect of deep discouragement and even falling away from the truth: "I have said these things to you to keep you from stumbling" (John 16:1). There is no explicit connection of troubles and discouragement and veering away from God—all prompted or orchestrated by the devil. Still, the devil lurks in the background of the Last Supper in John's Gospel. The devil has put it in the heart of Judas to betray Jesus (John 13:2). The devil arrives in the passion and death of Jesus: "I will no longer talk much with you, for the ruler of this world is coming. He has no power over me" (John 14:30). Jesus prays for his disciples: "I am not asking you to take them out of the world, but I ask you to protect them from the evil one" (John 17:15).

In his last discourse in John's Gospel, Jesus gives himself to his disciples as the source of their hope and encouragement. He alerts them to the coming struggles, which can breed discouragement. These struggles are to be expected. If the Lord and Master has been persecuted and has struggled, they will certainly follow in his footsteps because they are his servants and disciples. In the end, he is victorious. He triumphs over the power of Satan. His victory, however, does not belong to him alone. It is the victory of his followers as well. It is the victory that enables them to *take courage*. It is the victory that becomes the reference point in all future struggles, especially with the evil one.

The Responses to Discouragement: Common Directions

As we have considered some responses in the New Testament to the discouragement that the devil can use to move us away from God, certain common elements have become apparent. The letters of Paul, the Letter to the Hebrews, the Book of Revelation, and the Gospel of John represent a diversity of circumstances. Paul writes in the context of his mission and ministry. The Letter to the Hebrews addresses Christians who have become wearied as they try to live out their commitment. The book of Revelation speaks to Christians under the fire of perse-cution that threatens to destroy them. The Gospel of John and, in particular, its presentation of the Last Supper, addresses the future of the disciples of Jesus after his departure from them. The diverse per-spectives of these writings, however, eventually converge in a set of common messages to Christians who struggle with discouragement and the temptation induced by the evil one to fall away from the path to God. At least four such messages clearly emerge in these holy writings:

- **Expect struggles and discouragement.**
  Those who decide to follow Jesus will inevitably encoun-ter struggles and, with them, a spirit of discouragement. This should come as no surprise. Indeed, it is something to be anticipated. Only the spiritually naïve would expect things to be otherwise.

- **Expect the presence of the evil one to exploit our discouragement.**
  The background presence of the devil is more or less explicitly noted in the passages we have considered. In addition to the struggles that Christians find in trying to live out their commitment to the Lord, they also discover a hostile and adversarial presence that seeks to exploit their discouragement and to thwart their journey to God. Again, this is something to be expected. It is not an ex-traordinary phenomenon or experience but rather a part of the disciple's journey.

- **Hold to confidence.**
  Clearly, the confidence to which the passages summon us does not rest in our capacity to overcome struggles and discouragement. In fact, we are quite unable to meet the challenges posed by these struggles and this discourage-ment. Our confidence rests on the foundation of the victory of Jesus Christ, who brings life out of death and leads us to the glory of God. Paradoxically, the victory of

Jesus is most manifest on the cross, which seems to be the sign of defeat. The blood of the Lamb seals Jesus Christ's victory over sin, death, and the devil. True confidence means holding fast to him who is the victor.

- **Stay the course on pilgrimage.**
  Jesus Christ has conquered sin, death, and the devil. In faith, we are fully assured of this fact that enables our confidence in the face of struggles and discouragement. His definitive victory, however, does not signal the end of our struggles and encounters with discouragement while we remain on our earthly pilgrimage. With the whole of creation, we are moving toward the consummation of our destiny in God. We are not there yet. We are on pilgrimage. The horizon that frames our destiny is glory. In the meanwhile, we journey and struggle under the banner of the victory of Jesus Christ. Paul has words to this effect: "We know that the whole creation has been groaning in labor pains until now; and not only the creation, but we ourselves, who have the first fruits of the Spirit, groan inwardly while we wait for adoption, the redemption of our bodies. For in hope we were saved" (Romans 8:22–24).

These fundamental elements of response to discouragement lead us to focus on Jesus Christ. Whatever the perspective or circumstance, he and his victory establish the constant and consistent point of reference for our journey. This leads us to a concluding reflection on Jesus on the cross and his cry of abandonment. Here, at the cross and in his prayer of abandonment, we find ourselves drawn most deeply and most starkly into the mystery of struggle and victory.

Jesus in Abandonment: Victorious Confidence in God

If we keep our eyes fixed on Jesus, we can enter into the great struggle with discouragement, not just as a feeling but as the assault of the devil. The particular place where we can see him and hear him is on the cross as Mark's Gospel depicts it. The Gospel reads:

> At three o'clock Jesus cried out with a loud voice, "Eloi, Eloi, lema sabachthani?" which means, "My God, my God, why have you forsaken me?" . . . Then Jesus gave a loud cry and breathed his last. And the curtain of the temple was torn in two, from top to bottom. Now when the centurion who stood facing him saw that in this way he breathed his last, he said, "Truly this man was God's Son!" (15:34, 37–39)

Across the history of biblical interpretation, many commentators have attempted to understand these words of Jesus, which he draws from Psalm 22:2. Very often, they have been unable to accept the literal meaning of Jesus' prayer to express the feeling of abandonment by God, whom he has invoked in the language of intimacy as his *Abba*, Father. Some conclude that to accept these words literally would indicate that Jesus had lost hope, that he had truly despaired.

Raymond Brown has summarized the scholarly debate and concluded that the words of Jesus can be taken literally in their expression of a feeling of being forsaken as the Psalm quote indicates. He writes:

> Jesus is praying, and so he cannot have lost hope; calling God "My God" implies trust. Because he saw how Jesus died, the Marcan centurion confesses that Jesus was God's Son; Mark could not have meant that Jesus' despair prompted such a recognition. Thus, despair in the strict sense is not envisaged. Rather the issue is whether the struggle with evil will lead to victory; and Jesus is portrayed as profoundly discouraged at the end of his long battle because God, to whose will Jesus committed himself at the beginning of the passion . . . has not intervened in the struggle and seemingly has left Jesus unsupported. (That this is not true will become apparent the second that Jesus dies, for then God will rend the sanctuary veil and bring a pagan to acknowledge publicly Jesus' divine sonship.) Jesus cries out, hoping that God will break through the alienation he has felt.[11]

If we accept Brown's conclusions, the Gospel puts us into the state of profound discouragement that Jesus felt in the hour of his death.

The text also offers clues that indicate the presence of the evil one or the demonic in this moment and in this experience. The final battle with evil is enacted on the cross. The cry of Jesus and the giving up of his breath are associated with the victory over demonic forces. For example, we read in Paul's Second Letter to the Thessalonians: "And then the lawless one will be revealed, whom the Lord Jesus will destroy with the breath of his mouth" (2:8).

At the moment of death and facing the seemingly overwhelming and irresistible forces of evil, Jesus is brought to the depths of discouragement. Were he simply a human being, he could be subject to despair and surrender into hopelessness. In fact, what he does is quite different. Through his prayer he expresses both the real sense of abandonment and discouragement and the continuing and trusting relationship with God—*My God, my God*. In that prayer, he surrenders not into hopelessness but into the hands of his Father. And that is the version of Jesus' last words that Luke gives us: "Father, into your hands I commend my spirit" (23:46). Especially in Mark's version, the struggle and the victory over the evil one take place before and in Jesus' death. It is, however, a victory gained precisely because of the complete surrender in trust to *My God, my God*. And the victory already gained is evident only after the death of Jesus, who with his dying breath has slain the lawless one.

If, as indeed is the case, we are to replicate the death of the Lord in our own dying, then the implications of Jesus' cry on the cross are truly momentous for us. Our own struggle with deep discouragement, whether at the hour of death or in some more mitigated form before the hour of our death, puts us in vulnerable combat with the evil one. How we respond is of paramount importance. In Jesus on the cross, we find the pattern for his disciples and friends. The starkness of the prayer coupled with the lack of a guarantee that "things will feel better" makes this an extraordinary challenge. We cannot respond from our own resources, but only from God's grace already won for us in Jesus Christ, victor over sin and death. Our free cooperation with

God's grace enables us to move through but not necessarily beyond the experience of deep discouragement. We do so on a path of trusting surrender. It is the Lord who shows us the way, and it is also his saints who show us. The great Thérèse of Lisieux and the great Mother Teresa of Calcutta both experienced the darkness and the discouragement of the cross until the last moments of their lives.[12] Both surrendered in loving trust and came to share in Christ's victory.

In the end, for Jesus and Thérèse and Teresa, there is only the prayer. There are no feelings of consolation and, certainly, no feelings of triumph. There is only the prayer. It is the prayer that signals connection—*My God, my God*. Making the connection in prayer is the act of trust and entrustment. The prayer is the victory, although the victory is yet to be revealed. The prayer vanquishes the evil one.

The biblical tradition recognizes this pure trust that does not depend on feelings of consolation or assurance but only on the prayer itself. Psalm 88, titled a prayer for help in despondency, is an extraordinary example of this prayerful movement to God. The Psalmist moves through discouragement to reach out to God. Some selections from the Psalm:

> O Lord, God of my salvation, when, at night, I cry out in your presence, let my prayer come before you; incline your ear to my cry. . . . For my soul is full of troubles, and my life draws near to Sheol. I am counted among those who go down to the Pit; I am like those who have no help, like those forsaken among the dead, like the slain that lie in the grave, like those whom you remember no more, for they are cut off from your hand. . . . But I, O Lord, cry out to you; in the morning my prayer comes before you. O Lord, why do you cast me off? (vv. 1–5, 13–14)

In the midst of desolation and discouragement, there is the prayer, the cry to the Lord. Here is the living connection that fosters hope, even if hope is not felt. Here is the act of entrustment and surrender. This stark, perhaps even frightening path is the surest way to victory over the evil one—the way of loving, trusting, complete surrender. It represents, I would assert, the exact opposite of everything the devil is and stands for.

Although there has been much speculation, we do not know with exactitude what sin caused the angels to fall. We know that they did fall and that ever since they have wanted to bring humanity with them into ruin, into everything that is not God. Perhaps there is a clue to knowing their sin in the temptation, the original temptation that the devil presented to Adam and Eve. His offer was irresistible: "You will be like God" (Genesis 3:5). It is the temptation to self-assertion, to control one's destiny, to be totally and in an isolated fashion oneself and nothing else. It drew Adam and Eve away from loving surrender in confident trust. And sadly, it worked. Because it worked so well, there was fixed an unbridgeable gap, indeed, a chasm so wide no human could span or close it. It was the Son of God who made peace and reestablished the bridge between humanity and God. He did so in the only way that it could be done—in total, loving self-surrender, in abandonment on the cross: "My God, my God." And he stood victorious over the evil one. And ever since, it has been our possibility to stand victorious with him.

Conclusion

You know the message he sent to the people of Israel, preaching peace by Jesus Christ—he is Lord of all. That message spread throughout Judea, beginning in Galilee after the baptism that John announced: how God anointed Jesus of Nazareth with the Holy Spirit and with power; he went about doing good and healing all who were oppressed by the devil, for God was with him. (Acts 10:36–38)

When Peter proclaimed the good news of Jesus Christ to the Roman centurion in the tenth chapter of the Acts of the Apostles, he spoke a narrative of grace. Peter explained how God had visited his people and saved them from sin and death in his son Jesus Christ, crucified and risen from the dead by the power of the Holy Spirit. Whenever the good news is proclaimed, it must—by its very nature as good news—clearly speak of the greatness of God's gift in Jesus Christ, our salvation. At the same time, with sober realism we recognize with Peter that we are saved from evil and the evil one: "healing all who were oppressed by the devil." And until the end time when salvation and redemption in Jesus Christ take full hold of us, body and soul, and take full hold of our world that groans in travail and hope, we struggle with evil and the evil one. In that fact, we find the reason why the Lord bequeathed to us his prayer that concludes: "lead us not into temptation but deliver us from evil."

The last words of any prayer, but particularly of the Lord's Prayer, have a particular power and poignancy. The last words give us a final and concluding note as well as a petition that colors every other petition that preceded it within that prayer. And it may seem strange or puzzling to us that the prayer concludes as it does. We follow the version of the Lord's Prayer from Matthew's Gospel. It is the version the

Church uses in its prayer and liturgy. The New Revised Standard translation reads: "And do not bring us to the time of trial" (or alternately, "temptation") "but rescue us from the evil one" (or alternately, "from evil"). Pope Benedict XVI, in agreement with many commentators, explicates these last two petitions of the Lord's Prayer in his book *Jesus of Nazareth*:

> In the next-to-last petition the *not* sets the dominant note (do not give the Evil One more room to maneuver than we can bear). In the last petition we come before the Father with the hope that is at the center of our faith: "Rescue us, free us!" In the final analysis, it is a plea for redemption. What do we want to be redeemed from? The new German translation of the Our Father says *"vom Bösen,"* thus leaving it open whether "evil" or "the Evil One" is meant. The two are ultimately inseparable.[1]

Claiming an enlightened and modern attitude toward religious matters, many Christians have eliminated references to the devil or marginalized references to him to avoid embarrassment in our highly secularized milieu. Still, we cannot escape the Lord's Prayer and its very direct, very explicit references to freedom from temptation and deliverance from the evil one. As often as we offer this prayer that Jesus gives us, we acknowledge the uncomfortable fact that our lives are engaged in a struggle that is not yet finished. We may have confidence and hope in sharing in Jesus' victory, but still we struggle and know that there are no guarantees, no clear-cut assurances. As often as we pray the Lord's Prayer, we side with a clearheaded Christian realism. We believe that God created a good world. And we believe that that world has been marked by sin and, therefore, struggle. In the end, we believe that our world and we ourselves have been redeemed in Jesus Christ in a way that will be fully manifest at the end of time. "When all things are subjected to him, then the Son himself will also be subjected to the one who put all things in subjection under him, so that God may be all in all" (1 Corinthians 15:28).

There are many ways to understand the Lord's Prayer, and two thousand years of Christian tradition amply demonstrate many good interpretations and applications of this foundational prayer. In our context of understanding the struggle of the Christian life and our confrontation with the devil who deceives, divides, diverts, and discourages, I would suggest a particular way of seeing and understanding the Lord's Prayer.

When we pray as Jesus taught us, we join him in his struggle, the struggle that spans his temptations in the desert to his agony in the garden of Gethsemane to his sense of abandonment on the cross. Jesus prayed earnestly to be freed of temptation and to be delivered from the evil one, and God heard him.

> For we do not have a high priest who is unable to sympathize with our weaknesses, but we have one who in every respect has been tested [tempted] as we are, yet without sin. . . . In the days of his flesh, Jesus offered up prayers and supplications, with loud cries and tears, to the one who was able to save him from death, and he was heard because of his reverent submission. Although he was a Son, he learned obedience through what he suffered; and having been made perfect, he became the source of eternal salvation for all who obey him. (Hebrews 4:15; 5:7–9)

When we pray, "Our Father," we hear the devil's cynical words echo in the open desert: "If you are the Son of God, command these stones to become loaves of bread. . . . If you are the Son of God, throw yourself down" (Matthew 4:3, 6). Precisely because he is the loyal, loving son of the Father, he pushes aside the devil's suggestions. In the hour of testing in the garden of Gethsemane, Jesus calls on his Father and prays, "My Father, if it is possible, let this cup pass from me; yet not what I want but what you want" (Matthew 26:39). And on the cross, tested to the utmost, he does not abandon his Father but rather calls out to him, "My God, my God, why have you forsaken me?" (Matthew 27:46). For us to pray "Our Father" is to stay with Jesus in the struggle and to hold fast as God's beloved sons and daughters.

When we pray, "Our Father, who art in heaven," we lift our hearts to that place, that blessed state to which we aspire and to which we have not yet arrived. When we pray in his words, we are once again with Jesus, the victor over the struggle, who has gone to heaven but prays for us who remain on earth until heaven opens for us: "And now I am no longer in the world, but they are in the world, and I am coming to you. . . . I am not asking you to take them out of the world, but I ask you to protect them from the evil one" (John 17:11, 15).

We pray, "hallowed be thy name," and we are once again with Jesus as he struggles in the face of his impending death: "Now my soul is troubled. And what should I say—'Father, save me from this hour'? No, it is for this reason that I have come to this hour. Father, glorify your name" (John 12:27–28). With Jesus we learn to pray in all circumstances but most especially in the time of testing and trial in our struggle with the forces of evil and death to glorify God's name, to let it be blessed. This prayer evokes the prayer of the just man Job, whom Satan oppressed. Job prayed "The Lord gave, and the Lord has taken away; blessed be the name of the Lord" (Job 1:21).

We pray, "thy kingdom come" in the words that Jesus gave us. Once more, we hear the devil's words tempting Jesus in the desert: "Again, the devil took him to a very high mountain and showed him all the kingdoms of the world and their splendor; and he said to him, 'All these I will give you, if you will fall down and worship me'" (Matthew 4:8–9). The devil continues to tempt us with the illusory and passing kingdoms of this world. With Jesus, we set our hearts on the kingdom that will never end, because it is God's kingdom. His reign and his sovereignty, we pray, will take over every other claim that is made on our lives and the world that we live in. And we know, in Jesus, that this kingdom comes about through the power and the struggle of the cross on which was affixed the charge: "This is Jesus, the King of the Jews" (Matthew 27:37). Only a crucified king can usher in the kingdom of God, and only a people joined to him on the cross can enter that kingdom and triumph over "the cosmic powers of this present darkness" (Ephesians 6:12).

We pray, "Thy will be done on earth as it is in heaven." In the course of Jesus' temptations, the devil tries to induce him to do what he might want to do—to turn stones into bread, to be the spectacular messiah who astonishes the crowds by casting himself from the Temple, or to gain easy access to earth's kingdoms by false worship. In each instance, Jesus resists. Implicitly but clearly in his refusal of the devil's offers, he defers to his Father's will. He does that again in the garden of Gethsemane: "not what I want but what you want" (Matthew 26:39). He bows to his Father's will on the cross. Jesus consciously embraces the Father's will as the sustaining force of his life: "My food is to do the will of him who sent me and to complete his work" (John 4:34). This ready availability to do the Father's will characterizes his whole life, culminating with the offering of his very body in sacrifice on the cross, as the Letter to the Hebrews describes it: "When Christ came into the world, he said, 'Sacrifices and offerings you have not desired, but a body you have prepared for me. . . . See I have come to do your will.' And it is by God's will that we have been sanctified through the offering of the body of Jesus Christ once for all" (10:5, 9–10). We who are tempted and tested continue to pray with Jesus, "Thy will be done on earth as it is in heaven."

We continue to pray, "Give us this day our daily bread." Bread is not only sustenance; it can also be the stuff of temptation: "He fasted forty days and forty nights, and afterwards he was famished. The tempter came and said to him, 'If you are the Son of God, command these stones to become loaves of bread.'" In his response to the devil, Jesus cites Deuteronomy and says, "One does not live by bread alone but by every word that comes from the mouth of God" (Matthew 4:2–4). When we pray for our daily bread, we are, in effect, struggling with Jesus as he confronts the evil one. We struggle to identify what truly sustains us and keeps us alive. We are pulled to bread that is not bread but some surrogate, a substitute in some form that may help for a while but does not last. It is not the imperishable bread that leads to eternal life, the bread that the Son gives (John 6:27). We are struggling when we pray for our daily bread, struggling to receive and accept "the true bread," that is, the bread that is truth, so that we can live not just for today but forever (John 6:32, 58).

We pray, "Forgive us our trespasses as we forgive those who trespass against us." A fundamental human struggle is a cycle of hurt followed by vengeful vindication followed by more vengeance. Jesus breaks this cycle on the cross. Explicitly in Luke's Gospel, he forgives those who crucify him: "Father, forgive them; for they do not know what they are doing" (23:34). Even more, his self-sacrificial gift on the cross opens the floodgates of forgiveness: "This is my blood of the covenant, which is poured out for many for the forgiveness of sins" (Matthew 26:28). When we pray for forgiveness and, at the same time, commit ourselves to the path of forgiveness, we join with Jesus in a movement of compassionate mercy that breaks the demonic cycle of retribution: "Love your enemies. . . . You will be children of the Most High; for he is kind to the ungrateful and the wicked. Be merciful, just as your Father is merciful. . . . Forgive, and you will be forgiven" (Luke 6:35–37).

We arrive again at the last petitions of the Lord's Prayer: "Lead us not into temptation but deliver us from evil [from the evil one]." As we pray in the words that Jesus gave us, we pray and struggle with him. We ask that the testing or temptation not overwhelm us. And we ask to share in his victory over the evil one who would take us away from God.

Every day, we raise this prayer to God. Every day, we acknowledge our struggle. It is not just a struggle with ourselves, but with the powers and principalities. It is a struggle with the evil one who wants us on a path of deception, division, diversion, and discouragement. It is the path away from God. Every time we raise this prayer, we do so with Jesus, who has known our struggle with the evil one, who has conquered all evil, and who enables us to share in his victory:

> If we have died with him, we will also live with him;
> if we endure, we will also reign with him. (2 Timothy 2:11–12)